WHAT IS "BAPTIZED IN HOLY SPIRIT"?

THE MEANING OF "EATING MY FLESH AND DRINKING MY BLOOD" IN JOHN 6:5-61

THE LORD JESUS CHRIST WASHING THE FEET OF HIS TWELVE APOSTLES (JOHN 13:17)

THE NON-LITERAL MEANING OF WATER IN THE NEW TESTAMENT SCRIPTURES

FIRST PUBLISHED:2012

By: A scribe discipled into the kingdom of the heaven

Other books by the same author

Book No. 1 – One God existing in 3 Persons – Is this the God according to the bible? First Published: 2013

Book No. 2 – Teachings of Jesus Christ – First Published: 2011

Book No. 3 – Summary of some key teachings of the Lord Jesus Christ – First Published: 2013

Book No. 4 – Divorce and remarriage in relation to the gospel of salvation for believers into Christ Jesus – First Published: 2011

Book No. 5 – Two important Greek words frequently used by the Lord Jesus Christ and His disciples in their teachings and preaching concerning "poieo" and "ergazomai"
First Published: 2013

Book No. 6 – Works or "Ergon"(meaning works or toils or acts) in relation to the gospel of salvation – First Published: 2011

Book No. 7 – The gospel of salvation – the difficult journey to find everlasting life – Version One and Version Two. The gospel of salvation as taught by Paul. First Published: 2011

Book No. 8 – The teachings of Paul based on the cornerstone teachings of Jesus Christ – First Published: 2012

Book No. 9 – The significance of the differences between old creation and new creation. What is the meaning of salvation according to the bible? The resurrection and transformation to everlasting life and to everlasting death. All new testament saints must walk as new creation. First Published: 2011

Book No. 10 – The seven prophecies of the Lord Jesus Christ regarding the kingdom of the God and the gospel of salvation and what will happen with the passage of time in Matthew chapter thirteen – First Published: 2011

Book No. 11 – Seven letters to the seven churches in Asia (revelation chapters two and three)

Book No. 12 – The importance of the word "good" in the new testament scriptures – First Published: 2012

Book No. 13 – The God is the standard for all true believers into Christ Jesus. Righteous men and the prophetic word of the God. Followers of the Lord Jesus Christ must be made perfect, holy, righteous and good in order for them to receive everlasting life. First Published: 2013

Book No. 14 – What did Jesus do and teach about Sabbath? Circumcision – its importance in old testament days and its relevance in new testament days. First Published: 2012

Book No. 15 – What did Paul teach regarding the law of the God(or the law of Moses) in relation to the gospel of salvation? First Published: 2013

Book No. 16 – Understanding the book of revelation(excluding chapters two and three) – First Published: 2011

Book No. 17 – Baptisms in new testament scriptures. Table of Lord. First Published: 2013

Book No. 19 – What the bible teach about creation of mankind and other creatures and what happened to mankind after creation First Published: 2011

Book No. 20 – Is the church the bride of Christ? Is Jesus Christ a biological descendant of David? Jesus Christ was the last Adam and not the second Adam as many falsely preached. The first man and the second man. First Published: 2013

Book No. 21 – The five Greek words in the new testament scriptures relating to holy, holiness and to be made holy. First Published: 2012

Book No. 22 – Who is a Christian? How do we know we belong to the Lord Jesus Christ? Is it important to hear the voice of the Lord Jesus Christ? How can a believer hear the voice of the Shepherd (or Pastor), the Lord Jesus Christ in order to follow Him? First Published: 2011

Book No. 23 – What do the new testament scriptures teach concerning the Greek word "krino" translated as "judge(d)"?
First Published: 2013

Book No. 24 – Scriptures relating to salvation by the Lord Jesus Christ – First Published: 2013

Book No. 25 – Love("agape"), the love("agape") and to love ("agapao") in the new testament scriptures – First Published: 2012

Book No. 26 – Biblical meaning of the translated words truth and the truth in the new testament scriptures – First Published: 2013

Book No. 27 – Some truth revealed by the Lord Jesus Christ that are important to believers into Christ – First Published: 2013

Book No. 28 – Are all believers called by the Lord Jesus Christ to carry out the Great Commission? Prophecies concerning the total contamination of the gospel. Many are called but few chosen.
First Published: 2014

Book No. 29 – The biblical meaning of the translated words "faith" and "the faith" and its importance in the gospel of salvation according to the New Testament Scriptures – First Published: 2016

Book No. 30 – Why the need for mankind to be saved? Would/will the God call all mankind to salvation? Biblical meaning of called, invited and chosen(election) to salvation – First Published: 2016

Book No. 31 – The church and churches according to the new testament scriptures comparing to the existing church and churches in the world

About the Author

The author in understanding Matthew 13:52 is just a scribe discipled into the kingdom of the heaven. As a scribe, he was/is led to write since 2003 as much as was/is revealed to him concerning the gospel, the kingdom of the God from the Old Testament and New Testament Scriptures. The author continues to remain a scribe discipled into the kingdom of the God. The author ceases to reveal his name as we are in the last days of the prophecies of the parable of the Concealed Treasure(Matthew 13:44) and the parable of the Extremely Valuable Pearl(Matthew 13:45-46).

Terminology and Proper English Expression

All the writings in all the books of the scribe(discipled into the kingdom of the heaven) always place the translation and revelation of the true meaning of the Word of the God **above** Proper English Expression(which often distort the truth of the Word of the God).

The inclusion of such terminology as "the God" instead of "God"; or "Lord" instead of "the Lord"; or "the sin" instead of "sin"; or "the lawlessness" instead of "lawlessness"; or "the faith" instead of "faith"; or "the love" instead of "love"; or "the evil" instead of "evil", etc in the writings by the scribe are for the purpose of revealing the true meaning of scriptures. This will often be seen in the writing of the scribe and will often result in "not so Proper English Expression."

Ultimately, those who have adequate understanding of Scriptures, particularly the New Testament Scriptures will know the importance of **using correct terminology above** Proper English Expression, because in the translation from Greek to English if Proper English Protocol is to be followed, the true meaning according to the original Greek Texts may be lost or distorted.

This book is profitable and beneficial to those who are being called and to those already called by the God to salvation and especially to those who love the Lord Jesus Christ, the Son of the God.

This Book contains four booklets with titles:-
Booklet One – What does it mean to be "baptized in Holy Spirit"?
Booklet Two – The meaning of "Eating My flesh and drinking My blood" in John 6:5-61.
Booklet Three – The Lord Jesus Christ washing the feet of His twelve disciples(John 13:4-17).
Booklet Four – The non-literal meaning of water in the New Testament Scriptures. They are copyrights of Jasper International Pty. Ltd., Australia as Publishers.

All rights reserved. No portion of this book may be stored, reproduced in a retrieval system, or transmitted in any form or by any means, electronic, mechanical, photocopying, recording or otherwise without the prior permission of Jasper International Pty. Ltd., Australia.

This is Book number 18

First Published: 2012

References used:

Interlinear Greek-English New Testament Third Edition, Jay P. Green Sr. Published by Baker Books 2000.

Strong's Exhaustive Concordance of the Bible, James Strong, S.T.D. LLD. Published 1994 by World Bible Publishers.

The Holy Bible containing the Old and New Testaments New King James Version by Thomas Nelson Publishers.

PREFACE

This book is part of a series of separately titled books concerning the gospel of salvation and the kingdom of the God based on the CORNERSTONE teachings of the Lord Jesus Christ and the FOUNDATION teachings of the apostles and prophets.

This is Book number 18 and consists of four booklets, namely:-
Booklet One reveals the true meaning of "to be baptized in Holy Spirit."
Booklet Two reveals the true meaning of "Eating My flesh and drinking My blood" in John 6:5-61.
Booklet Three reveals the true meaning of the Lord Jesus Christ washing the feet of His twelve apostles in John 13:4-17.
Booklet Four reveals the true meaning of non-literal water in New Testament Scriptures.

There are two major different understanding of "baptism in Holy Spirit." On one side are "Christian groups" who believe that "baptism in Holy Spirit" is the same as "born from the Spirit" while on the other side are "Christian groups" who believe that "baptism in Holy Spirit" is different to "born from the Spirit." This is the reason for the release of Booklet One.

Many Roman Catholics and Lutherans believe that when the Lord Jesus Christ told the Jews to "eat His flesh and drink His blood" in John 6:5-61 it was in reference to the partaking of the Lord's Table. This is the reason for the release of Booklet Two.

There are "Christian groups" who practice the literal washing of feet of other "fellow Christians" to conform to the command of the Lord Jesus Christ in John 13:4-7. Is this practice in conformance to the true meaning of the Lord Jesus Christ' command? Booklet Three reveals the true meaning of the Lord's command to His disciples to wash each other's feet.

Booklet Four is included in this book to reveal the biblical meaning of the figurative usage of the word "water" in the New Testament Scriptures.

If believers are to be built into the unity of the faith they must all have the same understanding of all the commandments and teachings of the Lord Jesus Christ, otherwise any differences in understanding and practice of the commandments and teachings of the Lord Jesus Christ will lead to disunity and ultimately the total contamination of the gospel of salvation, which has already come to pass.

Every believer who reads this book is urged to test its content against the unadulterated word of the God, the original texts of the Bible in order to prove and/or to disprove its veracity.

TABLE OF CONTENT   **PAGE**

Booklet One – What does it mean to be baptized in Holy Spirit" according to Scriptures?

Introduction   7

The goal is to reveal the truth concerning "to be baptized in Holy Spirit"   8

Why is it not possible for the Holy Spirit to dwell in the apostles before the death, resurrection and glorification of Jesus Christ?   12

The issues that need to be resolved by Scriptures.   25

Booklet Two – The meaning of "Eating My flesh and drinking My blood" in John 6:5-61

Introduction   34

John 6:5-61   34

Booklet Three – The Lord Jesus Christ washing the feet of His twelve apostles in John 13:4-17

Introduction	60
What is the significance?	60
What is the message that the Lord Jesus Christ wanted to teach His apostles?	62
What then is the significance of washing feet?	66
Water represents the Word of the God	69

Booklet Four – The non-literal meaning of water in the New Testament Scriptures

Cleansing or purifying one from uncleanliness	72
The putting to death of the flesh	73
The Holy Spirit whom the Lord Jesus Christ promised	76
The Word of the God	78
Everlasting life	78
Appendix – Scriptures with word "water"	79

BOOKLET ONE

WHAT DOES IT MEAN TO BE "BAPTIZED IN HOLY SPIRIT" ACCORDING TO SCRIPTURES?

INTRODUCTION

There are two so-called Christian camps in regards to the meaning of "baptize in Holy Spirit." One camp of so-called Christians or Christian organizations believe that "to be baptized in Holy Spirit" is different from to "be born from the Spirit", while the other camp of so-called Christians or Christian organizations believe "to be baptized in Holy Spirit" is the same as to "be born from the Spirit." The former group of "Christians" believed/believe that all believers are/must be born from the Spirit and did/do not necessarily have to be baptized in Holy Spirit. To them, only when believers are baptized in Holy Spirit will they have the gifts("charisma") of the Holy Spirit such as speaking in tongues(languages), prophecy, healing, etc. And they know for sure a believer has been baptized in Holy Spirit when the believer is able to speak in tongue(language), prophesy, etc. The latter group of "Christians" believe that "baptism in Holy Spirit" is the same as to "born from the Spirit" but do not believe in the existence of the gifts("charisma") of the Spirit after the days of the 12 apostles. Yet there are also "Christians" who believe that unless believers are baptized in Holy Spirit and speak in languages(tongues) they are not saved.

The goal of this booklet is to reveal the truth concerning "to be baptized in Holy Spirit" - what is it and how does it relates to "be born from the Spirit"?

John the Baptist was the first man of the God to introduce the term "baptized in Holy Spirit." He said he baptized in water, but the One coming after him, that the Lord Jesus Christ will baptize in Holy Spirit and fire(Matthew 3;11; Mark 1:8; Luke 3:16 & John 1:33).

The Lord Jesus Christ confirmed what John the Baptist said when just before His ascension to the heaven to be seated at the right of His Father, He told His apostles, *"And behold! I sent forth the promise of My Father upon you. But you sit in the city of Jerusalem, until you are invested with power originating from on high..."* (Luke 24:49) unquote. This same incident was also reported in Acts 1:2-10, quote, verses 4 & 5, *"And having assembled together with them, He enjoined them not to depart from Jerusalem, but to await the promise of the Father, which you heard of Me, because John indeed baptized in water, but you will be baptized in Holy Spirit not many days* after *this."* unquote. Then in verse 8, quote, *"But you will receive power, the Holy Spirit supervening upon you; and you will be My witnesses in both Jerusalem and in all the Judea and Samaria, and until the end of the earth."* unquote.

So in Acts 2:1-12, on the day of Pentecost the apostles were filled with the Holy Spirit and began to speak in other languages(tongues) from different regions(centres) and not some babblings of no known languages. Each could speak a language(tongue) or languages(tongues) as given by the Holy Spirit, although those who spoke the languages might not know what languages they were, and what they meant; but others who came from the regions where the languages were spoken would understand.

Peter explained what happened was that having spoken by the prophet Joel in Joel 2:28-32; when the God will pour out His Spirit upon all flesh and some will see visions, some dream dreams and some prophesy and in Acts 2: 21, quote, *" And it will be, everyone, whoever may call on the name of Lord will be **saved**."* unquote – meaning those who turn to the Lord Jesus Christ are those who believe into Him will be **saved**. The ones being saved means the believers will receive the Holy Spirit to indwell them(meaning to be born originating from the Spirit). Acts 2:21 was quoted from Joel 2:32.

Joel 2:32 was also quoted by Paul in Romans 10:13. Romans 10:13 was the end result of Romans 10:8-12 when Paul talked about the "word of the faith" or "the gospel" which he proclaimed(Romans 10:8). So those who hear the preaching of the gospel or the word of the faith if they confess the Lord Jesus Christ with their mouth and believe in their heart that the God raised Jesus from the dead, they shall be **saved**. Because with the heart one believes into righteousness and with the mouth confesses into **salvation**(Romans 10:9, 10). For everyone who believes upon Him will not be put to shame(Romans 10:11) and *"For everyone who may call upon the name of Lord will be **saved**"*(Romans 10:13 – taken from Joel 2:32).

Romans 10:8-13 is the preaching of the gospel and those believing the gospel are those who believe into the Lord Jesus Christ and they will be **saved**. This is about **salvation**, just the same as Peter speaking in Acts 2:17-21, about what happened on the day of Pentecost. The apostles received the outpouring of the Holy Spirit, also known as being baptized in the Holy Spirit or being born originating from the Spirit and are being **saved**.

From Acts 2:1-21 and Romans 10:8-13 to be born originating from the Spirit is also the same as to be baptized in the Holy Spirit. The apostles followed the Lord Jesus Christ for about three and a half years and were already disciples of the Lord, that is they believed into the Lord Jesus Christ; now they received the indwelling of the Holy Spirit and they were born originating from the Spirit or being baptized in Holy Spirit. No one can receive the indwelling of the Holy Spirit until the Lord Jesus Christ is glorified(John 7:37-39) or until the Lord Jesus Christ is exalted to the right of the Father in heaven(Acts 2:32). This was what the Lord Jesus Christ told His disciples in John 14:17 - *"the Spirit of the truth whom the world is not able to receive, because they see Him not, nor know Him. But you know Him, because He remains from beside you and will be in you."* During the time when the disciples were with the Lord Jesus Christ while He was on the earth the first time as a man, the disciples had not received the Holy Spirit because Jesus Christ had not yet been glorified to the right of His Father in the heaven. Therefore when the Lord said that the Holy Spirit remains from beside His disciples in John 14:17, He meant that He(Jesus Christ) was from beside them and since the Holy Spirit dwelt in Jesus Christ, this meant the Holy Spirit was also from beside His(Jesus) disciples. But the Holy Spirit will one day be <u>in His disciples</u> and that day was on the day of Pentecost as revealed in Acts chapter two. Therefore this coming of the Holy Spirit upon the apostles on the day of Pentecost was the coming of the Holy Spirit to dwell in the hearts of the apostles, same as being called "baptized in Holy Spirit."

    We can safely say that anyone who died before the Lord Jesus Christ has ascended to the heaven and glorified at the right of His Father, can never be born originating from the Spirit or can never be baptized in the Holy Spirit or can never have the indwelling of the Holy Spirit when he was alive. Why? Because the promise of the Holy Spirit cannot be given until Jesus Christ has ascended to the heaven and glorified to the right of His Father in heaven.

Why is not possible for the Holy Spirit to dwell in the apostles before the death, resurrection and ascension of the Lord Jesus Christ to be glorified to the right of His Father, the God in the heaven?

The Holy Spirit is **holy** and He is also the Spirit of **the truth.** It is obvious that the **Holy Spirit of the truth** cannot dwell in **anyone** who is a sinner. A sinner is one who is unrighteous and evil. All mankind descended from Adam carry **the sin** in their flesh and are evil or unrighteous(Genesis 6:5; Genesis 8:21; Matthew 7:11; Luke 11:13; Matthew 12:34; Romans 5:12; Romans 7:114-24) and unless they are cleansed from their sins and the sin removed from their flesh and this cleansing from their sins and the sin in them removed can only happen when Jesus Christ had paid the penalty for their sins and remove the sin from them on the cross. And finally the Holy Spirit can only be given when the Lord Jesus Christ has ascended and glorified to the right of His Father, the God in the heaven to receive the promise of the Holy Spirit from His Father before the Holy Spirit can be given to dwell in all true believers into Christ.

The Lord Jesus Christ while He was on the earth was preaching about the Holy Spirit whom He said He will ask the Father that He may give the Holy Spirit to His disciples.

Let us go through all the incidents where the Lord taught about the Holy Spirit whom the Father will give through His Son, Jesus Christ.

1) Luke 11:13 – Accordingly, if you existing as evil know to give good gift to your children, how much more the Father originating from heaven will give Holy Spirit to the ones asking Him.

2) John 3:3, 5, 6, 7, 8
Jesus answered and said to him, Truly, truly I say to you, If not anyone be born from above, he is not able to see the kingdom of <u>the God</u>.
Jesus answered, Truly, truly, I say to you, If not anyone be born originating from water and Spirit, he is not able to enter into the kingdom of <u>the God</u>.
The one having been born originating from the flesh is flesh, and the one having been born originating from the Spirit is spirit.
Do not wander because I said to you, But you must be born originating from above.
The Spirit breathes when He desires, and you hear His voice; but you know not from where He comes, and where He goes. In this way is everyone who is born originating from the Spirit.

3) John 3:15, 16, 17, 18
In order that everyone believing into Him not perish, but have everlasting life.
For in this way, <u>the God</u> loved the world, so too His Son, the only begotten, He gave, in order that everyone believing into Him not perish, but have everlasting life.
For <u>the God</u> did not send His Son into the world in order that He judge the world, but in order that the world be saved through Him.

The one believing into Him is not condemned; but the one <u>not believing</u> already has been condemned, because he does not believe into the name of the only begotten Son of <u>the God</u>.

John 3:3, 5, 6, 7, 8 – the Lord told Nicodemus that one is not able to see the kingdom of <u>the God</u> if one is not born from above which means if one is not born originating from the Spirit. To be able to "see" means to be able to perceive or understand. So, unless one is born originating from the Spirit one will not be able to understand the kingdom of <u>the God</u>.

The kingdom of <u>the God</u> is synonymous with everlasting life. To inherit everlasting life is to enter into the kingdom of <u>the God</u>(Matthew 19:16, 23, 24, 25, 29; Mark 10:17, 23-26, 30; Luke 18:18, 24, 25, 26, 29, 30). And if one is not born originating from water and Spirit one will not be able to enter into the kingdom of <u>the God</u>. This means to inherit everlasting life one must be born originating from water and Spirit. Nicodemus could not understand what the Lord meant by being born originating from Spirit; less even to understand to be born originating from water and Spirit.

Finally, the Lord Jesus Christ spoke plainly to Nicodemus in John 3:15-18, that the God sent His Son, Jesus into the world and everyone <u>believing into Him</u> shall be <u>saved</u>. Those who do not believe are already condemned. So those who believe into Jesus Christ are those born originating from water and Spirit and will inherit everlasting life.

4) John 4:10, 13, 14, 15
Jesus answered and said to her, If you knew the gift of <u>the God</u>, and who is the One saying to you, Give Me to drink, you would have asked Him, and He would give to you living water.
Jesus answered and said to her, Everyone drinking originating from this water will thirst again,
but whoever may drink originating from the water which I will give him, will not ever thirst forever; but the water which I will give him will become a fountain of water in him, springing up into everlasting life.
The woman said toward Him, Lord, give me this water in order that I thirst not, nor come here to draw.

   In the above incident Jesus told the Samaritan woman if she knew the gift of <u>the God</u> and who is He speaking to her; she would ask Him and He would give her living water. The gift of <u>the God</u> is the Holy Spirit and Jesus is the One who has been authorized by <u>the God</u> to give the Holy Spirit, the living water.   The Holy Spirit will lead the believer into everlasting life. Although the Samaritan woman did not understand what Jesus was saying, she nevertheless believed Him and asked the Lord to give her the water so that she need not thirst anymore and need not have to return to the well to draw water again and again. Did Jesus give her the living water(Holy Spirit)? No! Jesus could not give her the Holy Spirit until He has fulfilled the Father's will on the earth and after He was raised from the dead and given everlasting life and after He has ascended to the heaven to be exalted and glorified to the right of His Father; then the Father will give Him the promise of the Holy Spirit.   To receive the Holy Spirit and not to thirst again means the Holy Spirit will lead the one given the Holy Spirit to everlasting life.

5) John 7:37-39
And in the last day of the great feast, Jesus stood and cried out, saying, If anyone thirst, let him come toward Me and drink.
The one believing into Me, even as the Writing said, Originating from his belly will flow rivers of living water. But He said this concerning the Spirit, whom the ones believing into Him were about to receive; for Holy Spirit was not yet(given), because Jesus was not yet glorified.

In John 7:37-39 – Jesus was referring to the same thing He spoke to the Samaritan woman in John 4:4-15 and to Nicodemus in John 3:3-21. This time Jesus spoke to the Jews. Whoever believes into Him will receive the Holy Spirit(living water). But at the time He was speaking to Nicodemus, the Samaritan woman and the Jews, the Holy Spirit could not be given yet because Jesus was not yet glorified. This means no one can be born again or born originating from Spirit as long as Jesus Christ has not yet fulfilled the works of the God(the will of the God) and has not yet ascended and glorified to the right of His Father in the heaven. Not even the thief who died with Him on the cross nor John the Baptist who died (before Jesus Christ had completed His works on the earth) were born originating from the Spirit.

That the Holy Spirit can only be given or poured out only after the Lord has ascended and glorified to the right of His Father in heaven is revealed in John 7:37-39; Acts 1:4, 5, 8 and confirmed in Acts 2:33.

Acts chapters 2 started with the outpouring of the Holy Spirit as promised by the Lord Jesus Christ in Acts 1:4, 5, 8. This led to the salvation firstly of the apostles, that is they were baptized in Holy Spirit, which means they were born originating from the Spirit; which led Peter to preach his first sermon to the Jews, that is the gospel of salvation (Acts 2:17-4).

Acts 2:33, *"Accordingly, being exalted to the right of <u>the God</u> and receiving the promise of the Holy Spirit from beside the Father, He poured out this which you now see and hear."*
This verse is the continuation of Peter's explanation of the outpouring of the Holy Spirit or the baptism of the Holy Spirit. The Holy Spirit was promised by the Lord Jesus Christ to the Samaritan woman(John 4:4-15) and to the Jews(John 7:37-39) and was told to Nicodemus(John 3:3-21) in relation to those who believe into Him will receive the Holy Spirit and eventually to receive everlasting life.

Acts 2:33 is the answer to John 7:39. John 7:39 says the Holy Spirit cannot be given until Jesus Christ is glorified. Acts 2:33 tells us that Jesus having ascended to the heaven and having been exalted and glorified at the right hand of <u>the God</u>, His Father. Then Jesus received the promise of the Holy Spirit from His Father; then poured the Holy Spirit upon His disciples, starting with His apostles.

This same promise of the Holy Spirit was also spoken by the Lord Jesus Christ to His disciples in John 14:16-18, 26; John 15:26-27 and John 16:7-15.

There is only <u>one giving or pouring of the Holy Spirit</u> and that is to be baptized in the Holy Spirit which is the same as being born originating from the Spirit. There is no such teaching as being born originating from the Spirit is for salvation and a separate experience of being baptized in the Holy Spirit or to receive power to live a victorious life. All the above Scriptures tell of only one giving of the Holy Spirit and that is for salvation.

6) Acts 2:38 – And Peter said toward them, Repent and be baptized each of you upon the name of Jesus Christ into forgiveness of sins; and you will receive the gift of the Holy Spirit.
Acts 2:39 – For the promise is to you and to your children, even to all the ones in a distance, as many as Lord <u>the God</u> of us shall call toward Himself.
    Acts 2:38 & 39 are confirmation of Peter's explanation of the baptism of the Holy Spirit and the first sermon he preached after he, himself received the baptism. Because the Jews believed in the gospel preached by Peter(Acts 2:37), Peter then told them how to be saved by being baptized upon the name of the Lord Jesus Christ, so that their sins may be forgiven and they will receive the gift of the Holy Spirit – meaning they will be born originating from the Spirit or be baptized in the Holy Spirit. For the promise of the gift of the Holy Spirit is to all whom <u>the God</u> shall call toward Himself. Anyone who receives the Holy Spirit(who is the gift of <u>the God</u>) shall be saved. This means anyone who is baptized in the Holy Spirit is born again and shall be saved.   So again, Acts 2:38-39 talk about salvation and the baptism of the Holy Spirit.

Thus to be baptized in the Holy Spirit is the same as being born originating from the Spirit.

7) Acts 10:43-48
v43 – To this Person all the Prophets witness, through His name everyone believing into Him will receive forgiveness of sins.
v44 – Peter was still speaking these words, the Holy Spirit fell upon all the ones hearing the Word.
v45- And the faithful from circumcision were astonished, as many as accompanying Peter, because the gift of the Holy Spirit was poured out upon the gentiles.
v46- For they heard them speaking in languages magnifying <u>the God</u>. At the time Peter answered,
v47- whether anyone can prevent the water that these not be baptized who received the Holy Spirit, even as we also?
v48 – And he commanded them to be baptized in the name of the Lord. At the time they asked him to stay over some days.

8) Acts 11:14-18
v14- who will speak utterances toward you, in which you and all your house will be <u>saved</u>.
v15- And in the commencement of my speaking, the Holy Spirit fell upon them, in the manner also upon us in the beginning.
v16- And I remembered the utterance of Lord, in the manner He said, John indeed baptized with water, but you will be baptized in Holy Spirit.

v17- Accordingly, if <u>the God</u> gave the same gift to them in the manner also to us who <u>believed</u> upon the Lord Jesus Christ; I and who was I to be able to prevent <u>the God</u>?
v18- And hearing these things, they held their peace and glorified <u>the God</u>, saying, Therefore <u>the God</u> also has given the gentiles <u>repentance into life</u>.

Acts 10:43-48 referred to the incident in which Peter was sent by the Lord Jesus Christ to preach the gospel to the gentiles(Cornelius and his household). As Peter spoke the word of <u>the God</u>, the Holy Spirit fell on Cornelius and all his household who were hearing the word of <u>the God</u> and they began to magnify <u>the God</u> in languages. Peter then baptized them in water upon the name of Jesus Christ.

Acts 11:14-18 was part of Peter's explanation to the church of Jerusalem why he went to preach to the gentiles. Acts 11:14 were the words spoken by Cornelius to Peter. Cornelius told Peter than an angel appeared to him (Cornelius) and told him to send for Peter "who will speak utterances to you in which you and all your house will be **saved**." This means Peter will preach the gospel to Cornelius and his household, in which they will be saved. To be saved means Cornelius and his household will be born originating from the Spirit. And this happened as Peter spoke the utterance of <u>the God</u> to Cornelius and his household, the Holy Spirit fell upon them and they began to magnify <u>the God</u> in languages.

Peter then explained to the church in Jerusalem, quote, *"And I remembered the utterance of Lord, how He said, John indeed baptized with water, but you will be baptized in Holy Spirit." (Acts 11:16).* So to be baptized in Holy Spirit is the same as being born originating from the Spirit, because Peter continued to explain in Acts 11:17-18, *"Accordingly, if <u>the God</u> gave the same gift to them in the manner as to us, **having believed** upon the Lord Jesus Christ, I and who was I to be able to prevent <u>the God</u>? And hearing these things, they held their peace and glorified <u>the God</u>, saying, Concluding therefore, <u>the God</u> also has given the gentiles **<u>repentance into life</u>**."*

Having believed, the gentiles received **<u>repentance into life</u>** – means having believed they were born from the Spirit and given repentance into life. So to be baptized in the Holy Spirit is the same as to be born originating from the Spirit is the same as to have the indwelling of the Holy Spirit.

9) Acts 15:7, 8, 9
v7- And much discussion have occurred, standing up, Peter said to them, Men, brothers, you understand that from days of old, <u>the God</u> chose out among us through my mouth the gentiles to hear <u>the word of the gospel</u> and to <u>believe</u>.
v8- and the heart knower of God, testified to them, giving them the Holy Spirit, even as also to us.
V9- and He distinguished nothing between both us and them, the faith having cleansed their hearts.

Acts 15:7-9 was part of the incident when Paul and Barnabas came to meet the apostles, elders and the church in Jerusalem to discuss the issue raised by some Jewish believers from Jerusalem who wanted the gentiles believers in Antioch to be circumcised. Peter told the congregation how he was chosen by <u>the God</u> to preach the gospel to the gentiles(Cornelius and his household – referring to the same incident in Acts 10:43-48 and Acts 11:14-18), that they might believe. <u>The God</u> gave the gentiles(Cornelius and his household) the gift of the Holy Spirit that they may be saved(the faith having cleansed their hearts). So Peter preached the gospel to Cornelius and his household, who hearing and believed and they were baptized in the Holy Spirit, that meant to be born originating from the Spirit and to receive salvation.

10) Acts 19:2-6
v2- And said toward them, Whether believing they have received the Holy Spirit. And they said toward him, But we did not hear there is Holy Spirit.
v3- Also he said toward them, According, into what were you baptized? And they said toward baptism of John.
v4- and Paul said, John indeed baptized a baptism of repentance to the people, saying, that they should <u>believe into the One coming</u> after him, that is, <u>into the Christ Jesus</u>.
v5- and hearing they were baptized into the name of the Lord Jesus.
v6- and Paul laying hands upon them, the Holy Spirit came upon them, and they spoke in languages and prophesized.

In this incident Paul met some disciples of John the Baptist and asked them if they have received the Holy Spirit. They were unaware of the Holy Spirit. They told Paul they received the baptism of John. Paul explained to them that the baptism of John is a baptism of repentance – telling the Jews to believe into Jesus Christ. Then Paul baptized them into the name of the Lord Jesus Christ and laid hands upon them and they spoke in languages and prophesized.

Notice Paul never use the words: "Baptized in the Holy Spirit" or "Born originating from the Spirit." He only talked about **receiving** the Holy Spirit or **indwelling** of the Spirit or **sealed** with the Holy Spirit – in all his teachings in his epistles.

Acts 19:2-6 is an incident where the disciples of John the Baptist who having believed in the Lord Jesus Christ were then baptized into the name of the Lord Jesus Christ and then received the Holy Spirit through the laying on of the hands by Paul. This is the same as they being baptized in the Holy Spirit, because they spoke in languages and prophesized. Paul **never** distinguish the difference between baptism in the Holy Spirit and born originating from the Spirit or receiving the Holy Spirit.

Paul was the one chosen by the Lord Jesus Christ to explain the full gospel in the New Testament, but he never mention the terms "baptized in the Holy Spirit" or "born originating from the Spirit." Yet Paul is the apostle who taught much about salvation through the preaching of the gospel.

Mostly, Paul preached the gospel, and those hearing and believing the gospel got saved. There is no distinction in the New Testament between being born originating from the Spirit and being baptized in the Holy Spirit or receiving the Holy Spirit or believing in the gospel or believing into the Lord Jesus Christ.

All who believe in the gospel, believe into the Lord Jesus Christ and will receive the indwelling of the Holy Spirit or being born originating from the Spirit or being baptized in the Holy Spirit.

This is the teaching of the New Testament Scriptures.

THE ISSUES THAT NEED TO BE RESOLVED BY SCRIPTURES ARE THESE:-

1) Does it mean that all who are born originating from the Spirit or baptized in the Holy Spirit must speak in languages(tongues) or prophesy?

2) Acts 8:12-17 – The Samaritans who believed the gospel preached by Philip and were baptized into the name of the Lord Jesus Christ, did not receive the Holy Spirit or baptized in the Holy Spirit until Peter and John arrive to lay hands on them. Were they not born originating from the Spirit after believing the gospel and baptized in the name of Jesus Christ?

3) Why did some receive the baptism of the Holy Spirit before water baptism in the name of Jesus Christ and some only after water baptism(in the name of Jesus Christ)?

Question 1 – Does it mean that all who are born originating from the Spirit or baptized in the Holy Spirit must speak in tongues(languages) or prophesy?

Scriptures teach that **not all** speak in tongues(languages) – 1 Corinthians 12:28, 30, quote, *"And the God placed in the church: firstly apostles, secondly prophets; thirdly, teachers; thereafter workers of power; then gifts of healings; reliefs, governing, kinds of languages(tongues). **Not all** have gifts of healings. **Not all** speak languages (tongues). **Not all** interpret."*

It is clear from the above two verses that not all true believers speak in languages(tongues). True believers are those who are born originating from the Spirit or baptized in the Holy Spirit.

However, the Book of Acts gives the impression that those who are baptized in the Holy Spirit spoke in tongues(languages) and/or prophesized – that was how they were recognized as having received the gift – the Holy Spirit. Why then did Paul teach that **not all speak in tongues**?

Does it mean that to be baptized in the Holy Spirit is not the same as being born originating from the Spirit? This is the conclusion and rationalization of those who believe in the distinction between being born originating from the Spirit and being baptized in the Holy Spirit.

But Scriptures have already shown that being born originating from the Spirit is the same as being baptized in the Holy Spirit – and much of this proof is also given in the Book of the Acts.

So how do we explain the apparent discrepancies of the observance in the Book of the Acts that all who were baptized in the Holy Spirit spoke in tongues(languages) and/or prophesized and yet in 1 Corinthians 12:28, 30 Paul taught that **not all speak in tongues**.

Again, Scriptures provide the answers. There is no contradiction in the word of <u>the God</u>. But human rationalization must not be involved in the explanation. Only the Holy Spirit can reveal the consistency of His word.

Before the Book of the Acts, no one has received the indwelling of the Holy Spirit except the Lord Jesus Christ. The Holy Spirit can only be given after the Lord Jesus Christ has ascended and glorified at the right hand of <u>the God</u> in the heaven. So when the Lord Jesus Christ first poured His Spirit upon His 12 apostles on the day of Pentecost, He must show them clear signs that they have received the gift("dorea"), the Holy Spirit whom He promised them(Acts 1:4, 5, 8). And the best way to reveal to the apostles and the rest of the people proof when they received the Holy Spirit is for the Holy Spirit to display His gifts("charisma") which the Holy Spirit gives to those whom He indwells. The Holy Spirit is the gift("dorea") from <u>the God</u>. Those who have the Holy Spirit dwelling in them, the Holy Spirit will distribute to each believer one or more gifts("charisma" - such as word of wisdom, word of knowledge, faith, gifts of healing, workings of power, discerning of spirits, kinds of languages(tongues), and interpretation of tongues – 1 Corinthians 12:7-11). In the case on the day of Pentecost, when the Lord Jesus Christ poured out the Holy Spirit upon His apostles, the Holy Spirit decided to distribute and display <u>immediately</u> the gifts("charisma") of tongues(languages) and prophecies. Of all the gifts("charisma") from the Holy Spirit, tongues and prophecies can be <u>immediately</u> manifested or displayed.

These are the two gifts("charisma") chosen by the Holy Spirit to display and manifest in the apostles and subsequently to other believers to let them and the rest of the people know as proof that they have received the gift("dorea") of the Holy Spirit. When the Lord Jesus Christ received the Holy Spirit on rising up from the water baptism by John the Baptist, He did not display the gift("charisma") of tongues or prophecies, because <u>the God</u> chose to reveal the coming of the Holy Spirit upon His Son, Jesus Christ through John the Baptist; and that was also how <u>the God</u> revealed to John the Baptist whom Jesus Christ is. So when the Holy Spirit fell on the apostles the Holy Spirit gave them the gifts("charisma") of speaking in tongues(languages) and prophecy; and they all spoke in tongues(languages) to display the gift ("charisma"), then they knew that they have received the Holy Spirit. <u>The God</u> also chose Peter to open the kingdom of <u>the God</u> to all peoples of the world; firstly to the Jews, secondly to the Samaritans and finally to the Gentiles. And the gift("dorea") of the Holy Spirit is given through the laying on of hands by His apostles, and later all those whom the Lord Jesus Christ chooses as "sent out ones" or "apostolos." The Book of the Acts also show that the Holy Spirit is given by the laying on of hands and this is done only after the preaching of the gospel; those hearing with understanding and believing were then immersed(baptized) in water into the name of Jesus Christ; and on arising from the water baptism the apostles laid hands on them to receive the Holy Spirit. The significance of water baptism into the name of the Lord Jesus Christ before the laying on of hands to receive the Holy Spirit is to follow the preaching of the gospel.

The gospel becomes the power of salvation to those believing that they were also crucified with the Christ and died on the cross, that is they were baptized into His death. Only when they were baptized into His death can they be baptized in the Holy Spirit – only when the old creation dies can the new creation be born. This is the significance of water baptism before the laying on of hands to receive the Holy Spirit. The Holy Spirit living in the believer represents the Lord Jesus Christ(John 14:26) and is the new creation. Therefore, if one does not believe that he also died with Christ on the cross, water baptism has no meaning, so is the laying on of hands.

    Thus when the apostles laid hands on those who have arisen from water baptism, the manifestation of tongues will reveal that the believers have received the Holy Spirit or have been baptized in Holy Spirit – this is necessary because it is such a new phenomenon – the baptism of the Holy Spirit. Actually, the Lord Jesus Christ also told His apostles in Mark 16:17, quote, *"And to the ones believing these signs will follow: they will cast out demons in My name; they will speak in new tongues(languages)..."* Here the Lord Jesus Christ was telling the apostles that those who believe into Him will receive the Holy Spirit and be given gifts("charisma") by the Holy Spirit, such as casting out of demons and speaking in new languages(tongues).

But later on the Holy Spirit through Paul in 1 Corinthians 12:28, 30 taught that not all who are baptized in the Holy Spirit or born originating from the Spirit will speak in tongues. But each believer will be given one or more gifts("charisma") by the Holy Spirit as He purposes.
This is the teaching of Scriptures on Baptism in Holy Spirit and Speaking in Tongues.

Question 2 – How does Scriptures reconcile Acts 8:12-17 where the Samaritans who heard and believed the gospel preached by Philip and were baptized(in water) in the name of Jesus Christ, but yet they did not receive the Holy Spirit? Does it mean that they were not born originating from the Spirit or baptized in the Holy Spirit?

Scriptures teach that wherever the Lord Jesus Christ is, there is the kingdom of the God(Luke 17:20 & 21). Therefore anyone who has the Lord Jesus Christ has the kingdom of the God. When the Lord Jesus Christ ascended to the heaven, the kingdom of the God is now represented by His Spirit or the Holy Spirit(John 14:26). The kingdom of the God is in everyone who has the indwelling of the Holy Spirit.

In Matthew 16:19, the Lord Jesus Christ told Peter that He will give Peter the keys of the kingdom of the heaven. So it is Peter who has the keys to the kingdom of the heaven. Peter preached the first sermon(gospel) to the

Jews in Acts 2:14-41, and 3000 souls were converted that day. That means the 3000 souls received the indwelling of the Holy Spirit or baptized in Holy Spirit or born originating from the Spirit. Peter opened the kingdom of the heaven to the Jews first. Then in Acts 8:5-13 Philip went to Samaria and preached the gospel to the Samaritans. He performed many signs and wonders and many believed in the gospel and the Lord Jesus Christ; they were then baptized(water immersion) in the name of the Lord Jesus Christ, yet they did not receive the Holy Spirit. It was only when Peter and John(Acts 8:14-17) went from Jerusalem to Samaria and laid hands on the baptized Samaritan believers that they received the Holy Spirit. Although nothing was said of their(Samaritan believers) speaking in tongues, this must have happened, otherwise Peter and John would not have straight away known that they had received the Holy Spirit. The Samaritans are not pure Jews and did not follow Judaism as practiced by the Jews. So Peter was the one who had the keys to open the door of the kingdom of the heaven to the Samaritan believers.

   Again, in Acts chapter 10, Peter was the one the Lord Jesus Christ called to open the kingdom of the heaven to the gentiles(Cornelius and his household). Thus as prophesized by the Lord Jesus Christ in Matthew 16:19, Peter was the one chosen by the Lord to open the door to the kingdom of the heaven to all peoples of the world, namely, the Jews and the Samaritans and the Gentiles. After that all those who are sent out by the Lord Jesus Christ to preach the gospel, when they lay hands on those believing the gospel and who have been baptized in the name of Jesus Christ will receive the Holy Spirit or baptized in the Holy Spirit or born originating from the Spirit.

Question 3 – Why did some receive the baptism of the Holy Spirit before baptism(in water) into the name of the Lord Jesus Christ?

The only incident of believers who received the Holy Spirit before baptism in water into the name of Jesus Christ is in Acts 10:44-48, regarding the salvation of Cornelius and his household. This is a special case because Cornelius and his household are gentiles. In the Old Testament days, gentiles are considered as dogs – unclean. During that time the Jews and even Peter were not given the full understanding that the God has now opened the door to the kingdom of the heaven or the door of the faith or the gospel to all peoples of the world including the gentiles. The Lord Jesus Christ had to show Peter and the Jews who accompanied him that the Holy Spirit is also being given to the gentiles, without Peter laying hands on Cornelius and his household – that is the God's desire to open the door to the kingdom of the heaven (ie door to salvation or to everlasting life) to the gentiles also. That was why Cornelius and his household received the Holy Spirit even without being baptized in water nor laying on of hands by Peter. Peter was the one chosen to preach the gospel to the gentiles. Once Cornelius and his household had received indwelling of the Holy Spirit, who is there to stop them from being baptized in water into the name of the Lord Jesus Christ.

All throughout the New Testament the process of receiving the Holy Spirit is:-
Preaching of the gospel by sent out ones from the Lord Jesus Christ.
Hearing and believing into the Lord Jesus Christ or believing in the gospel of salvation.
Followed by baptism in water into the name of the Lord Jesus Christ.
And followed by the laying on of hands on those believing by the sent out ones from the Lord Jesus Christ in order for the ones baptized in water to receive the Holy Spirit.

Scriptures teach that to be baptized in the Holy Spirit is the same as to be born originating from the Spirit is the same as to receive the gift("dorea") of the Holy, is the same as to receive the indwelling of the Holy Spirit, is the same as to be sealed with the Holy Spirit.

- END -

BOOKLET TWO

THE MEANING OF "EATING MY FLESH AND DRINKING MY BLOOD" IN JOHN 6:5 – 61

INTRODUCTION

Many Roman Catholics and the Lutherans have misinterpreted John chapter 6 relating to the eating of the flesh of Jesus Christ and drinking His blood to be part of the Lord's Table and this lie has for centuries indoctrinated the minds of millions of so called believers that even if the truth is explained – many will still find it difficult to get away from it – unless one is prepared to go to the Lord Jesus Christ and out of sincerity of the heart to tell the Lord Jesus Christ to erase all lies and false teachings especially in regards to this subject and opens one's eyes to see the truth by the revelation of the Holy Spirit.

JOHN CHAPTER SIX VERSES 5 - 61

Let us go through the whole of John chapter 6 and let the Holy Spirit reveal the truth – Scriptures interpreting Scriptures and put away our rational/intellectual carnal or fleshly mind.

The context of John chapter 6:-
John 6:1-13 - Jesus fed 5000 men – a true miracle. Jesus performed this miracle out of compassion and need for the people who had been following Him; for there was no where to buy so much food to feed such a crowd.

John 6:14, quote, *"Accordingly, the ones seeing what sign Jesus did say that this is truly The Prophet, the one coming into the world."* Unquote.
John 6:15, quote, *"Accordingly, knowing that they were about to come and seize Him in order that they might make Him king, Jesus withdrew once more to the mountains by Himself."* Unquote.

    The crowd having tasted the miracle which the Lord Jesus Christ performed was seeking for Him even more. Finally, they found Him across the sea.

John 6:25-26: - The crowd followed Him not because of the signs but for the food they ate and were satisfied. This means the crowd was only interested in the Lord Jesus Christ satisfying their needs of the old creation – which was what the crowd was only interested.

    That was why Jesus told them in John 6:27, quote, *"Do not labour(or toil) for food which perishes; but for the food enduring to everlasting life("zoe"), which the Son of the man will give to you; for <u>the God</u>, the Father stamped with a signet for preservation this One."* Unquote. This means to follow the Lord Jesus Christ requires labour and work.

    The crowd replied to the Lord Jesus Christ in John 6:28, quote, *"Accordingly, they said toward Him, What may we do in order that we may labour (or toil) the works of <u>the God</u>?* Unquote.

    Jesus answered them in John 6:29, quote, *"This is the work of <u>the God</u>, in order that you **believe into Whom** that One sent."* Unquote. The Lord Jesus Christ told the crowd to <u>believe into Him</u>. The meaning of "<u>believe into Him</u>" means to believe from beginning until the end of one's life-span on the earth.

The crowd being carnal or fleshly could not see the divine purpose of <u>the God</u>, but continued to pursue according to their carnal mind or fleshly thinking.

In John 6:30-31, quote, *"Accordingly, they said to Him. Certainly what sign do you do in order that we may see and **believe** You? What do You labour(or toil)? Our fathers ate the manna in the wilderness, even as it has been written: He gave them bread originating from the heaven to eat." (Psalms 78:24).* Unquote.

The Lord Jesus Christ had already performed a great miracle by feeding 5000 men from 5 barley loaves and two fish, and yet they were asking Him for another sign before they would **believe** Him. They quoted the miracles that happened for 40 years in the wilderness when their forefathers were fed with manna originating from the heaven. This indicated that the crowd wanted Jesus to continue to feed them to satisfy their flesh not just once, but continually. They were not interested in the divine purpose of <u>the God</u>, but only interested in satisfying the lust of their flesh. (So are so many so called Christians these days, who only want the Lord Jesus Christ to perform miracles every day to satisfy their flesh – who only want the Lord Jesus Christ to give them abundant life ("psuche") now on the earth – to satisfy their old creation – the flesh.)

Because the crowd brought up the subject of eating manna originating from the heaven, instead of **believing into Him** (which was what the Lord Jesus Christ told them to do in John 6:29), the Lord Jesus Christ had to respond accordingly, by saying in John 6:32, quote, *"Accordingly, Jesus said to them, Truly, truly I say to you, Moses did not give you the bread originating from the heaven, but My Father gives **you** the true bread originating from the heaven."* Unquote.

The Lord Jesus Christ tried to bring them back to the divine purpose of the God, that is to give them everlasting life, by first quoting Moses, when the crowd did not mention Moses(John 6:31). The Lord Jesus Christ told the crowd that it was not Moses who gave "**you**" the true bread originating from the heaven, but His Father gives "**you**" the true bread originating from the heaven. Notice the Lord Jesus Christ did not say, " it was not Moses who gave **your fathers** bread originating from the heaven, but My Father gave **your fathers** the true bread originating from the heaven." The Lord Jesus Christ used the word, "**you**" instead of "**your fathers**" because what the Lord Jesus Christ was saying to the crowd was that it was not the law of Moses that can give them everlasting life; but His Father is the One who gives them(crowd) the true bread(everlasting life) originating from the heaven. And that everlasting life is the Lord Jesus Christ Himself, who came down originating from the heaven; He is the true bread of life(everlasting). The Lord Jesus Christ was bringing the crowd to the present time in which He(Jesus Christ) who was sent by the Father originating from the heaven was the Bread originating from the heaven to give them everlasting life. John 6:33, quote, *"For the bread of <u>the God</u> is the One coming down originating from the heaven and giving life("zoe") to the world."* Unquote. The crowd's response to the Lord in John 6:34 shows that they did not understand the divine meaning of John 6:33. Their response to the Lord Jesus Christ was still of the carnal or fleshly mind. John 6:34, quote, *"Accordingly, they said toward Him, Lord **<u>always give us this, the bread</u>**."* Unquote. They wanted the Lord Jesus Christ to feed their flesh continually.

The Lord Jesus Christ tried to bring them back to the divine purpose of <u>the God</u> by answering them in John 6:35 & 36, quote, *"And Jesus said to them, I am the Bread of the Life("zoe"), the one <u>coming</u> toward Me not ever will hunger; and the one **<u>believing into Me</u>** not ever will thirst, never! But I say to you that you also have seen Me and **<u>did not believe</u>**."* Unquote.

Notice in John 6:35, Jesus said, "I am the Bread of the Life; the one coming toward Me not ever will hunger." Here Jesus used the words <u>coming toward Me</u> (and not <u>eating Me</u>). The one coming toward Jesus not ever will hunger – Jesus was not referring to natural or physical hunger. Then He said, "the one <u>believing into Me</u> not ever will thirst, never!" Here, Jesus used the words <u>believing into Me</u>(and not drinking My blood). Jesus was not referring to natural or physical drinking at all!

Those who follow the Lord Jesus Christ are those who <u>believe into Him</u> and they are His disciples. In John 10:27-28, Jesus said, quote, *"My sheep hear My voice, and I know them, and they follow Me. And I give them everlasting life, and they shall not ever perish forever,..."* Unquote.

    Therefore, the words, "not ever hunger" and "not ever thirst" mean that they will not ever perish forever. All mankind, even true disciples of the Christ must die or perish(first death), but those who follow Him or <u>believe into Him</u> will not ever die or perish forever. Because Jesus will raise them up from the dead in the last day to live forever or to give them everlasting life.

    Again in John 6:35 & 36 the Lord Jesus Christ repeated what He told the crowd what to do, as in John 6:29. He told them that those who **believe into Him** will not ever hunger or will not ever thirst; but He said they had seen Him and did **not believe**.

    The Lord Jesus Christ continued to speak to the crowd in John 6:37, 38 & 39, about those whom the Father gave to Him, He would not lose them, but will give them everlasting life, in reference to the 11 apostles; and that He came to do the will of His Father.

    Then in John 6:40, the Lord told the crowd what was the will of <u>the God</u>, quote, *"And this is the will of the One who having sent Me, in order that everyone seeing the Son and **believing into Him** have everlasting life and I will raise him up the last day."*

    He is the One who will give them everlasting life by raising them up from the dead in the last day, that is the day of resurrection.

As we have shown according to Scriptures, **believing into Him** means believing(or obeying) Him from beginning until the end of one's life-span.

Jesus already said that the crowd did not **believe** Him in John 6:36 – this is now revealed in John 6:41. John 6:41-42, quote, *"Accordingly, the Jews murmured concerning Him, because He said, I am the Bread, the One coming down originating from the heaven. And they said, Is this not Jesus, the son of Joseph whom we know the father and the mother? Accordingly, how this one says, I have come down originating from the heaven?"*

Let us look at how carnal or fleshly mind rationalizes:- John 6:9-13 – Jesus performed a miracle by feeding 5000 men from 5 barley and 2 fishes; the crowd was satisfied and said in John 6:14 - *"This is truly The Prophet, the One coming into the world."* Then in John 6:26-27 when Jesus spoke spiritual matters to them, they were not interested but kept asking for signs from Him. Then when Jesus again told them about spiritual matters(everlasting life) that He is the one coming down originating from the heaven and whoever **believes into Him** will have everlasting life, they started to murmur against Him; rationalised that how could He, whose father and mother they knew had claimed to have come down originating from the heaven. This is the danger. When we start to use our intellect/rational mind or carnal mind to analyse spiritual matters, we will never be able understand and see the truth; even if it is in our midst. Jesus Christ, the Son of the God was in their midst, but they could not see Him truly, but their natural mind see Him as the son of a carpenter.

The Lord Jesus Christ told the crowd not to murmur (John 6:43) and again told them in John 6:44-46 that no one is able to come to Him(Jesus) unless the Father drags him to Jesus Christ and the Lord Jesus Christ will give him everlasting life. This is an important key truth. Unless the God calls and chooses a person, he can never understand the truth and can never receive everlasting life. This is Scripture speaking – the word of the God – we have to accept it. It is the God Who calls and chooses, not anyone of us wanting to be saved.

Then in John 6:47, for the sixth time, Jesus told the crowd that *"the one **believing into Me** has everlasting life."*

So we see from John 6:29, 30, 35, 36, 40 & 47 the Lord Jesus Christ emphasized to the Jews that only those who **believe into Him** will have everlasting life. The Lord Jesus Christ could not convince the Jews to **believe into Him**, but if He does a miracle to satisfy their flesh, they will acknowledge Him as The Prophet Moses spoke of and even want to make Him their king.

WHY?   **Believing into Him** has many consequences – well explained in the 4 gospels of Matthew, Mark, Luke and John. **Believing into Him** means one must be His disciples. His disciples are His slaves and must follow Him. And to follow Him, His disciples must deny utterly themselves and pick up their crosses daily. His disciples must give up everything including themselves(souls) in order to be able to follow Him – and this is the only way for them to receive everlasting life(John 12:25). To have the new creation, the old must die(1 Corinthians 15:36) and this requires suffering in the flesh.

The Jews being in the flesh were not willing to give up their souls to follow Him. They only want miracles from Him to satisfy their old creation(flesh) on the earth that they might enjoy their life(soul) on the earth. As long as they were in the flesh they were fond of the flesh or themselves; they can never see the divine purpose of the God for them.

Because of their frame of mind, the Lord Jesus Christ had to speak to them in natural(soulish) terms, just as Paul told the Corinth believers, quote, *"But a natural(soulish) man receives not the things of the Spirit of the God, for they are foolishness to him, and he is not able to know, because they are spiritually discerned(1 Corinthians 2:14).*

"And brothers, I was not able to speak to you in the manner as to spiritual, but in the manner as to fleshly, as to infants in Christ. I gave you milk to drink and not food, for you are not yet able; but neither are you yet able now. For you are yet fleshly, ..."(1 Corinthians 3:1-3).
From John 6:27-47, the Lord Jesus Christ spoke to them the spiritual purpose of the God, but their carnal or fleshly mind could not accept nor understand. That was why the Lord Jesus Christ from John 6:48 to 58 started to speak to them as to fleshly as to infants or babes.
John 6:48, Jesus said, *"I am the Bread of the Life."*
John 6:49, Jesus said, *"Your fathers ate the manna in the wilderness and died..."*
John 6:50, Jesus said, *"This is the Bread, the One coming down originating from the heaven, in order that anyone may eat from it and not die..."*

John 6:51, Jesus said, *"I am the living Bread, the One coming down, originating from the heaven. If anyone eats from this, the Bread, he will live forever. And indeed the bread which I give is My flesh which I give on behalf of the life("Zoe") of the world."*
John 6:52, *"Accordingly the Jews disputed toward one another, saying, How is this One able to give up the flesh to eat?"*

    John 6:51 & 52 is the equivalence of what the Lord Jesus Christ said to the Samaritan woman at the well in John 4:10, 14, quote, *"Jesus answered and said to her, If you know the gift of <u>the God</u>, and who is the One saying to you, Give me to drink, you would have asked Him, and He would give you living water. But whoever may drink from the water which I give him will not ever thirst forever; but the water which I give to him will become a fountain of water, springing up into everlasting life."* Unquote.

    However, the response by the Jewish crowd in John chapter 6 was entirely opposite to the response of the Samaritan woman to the Lord Jesus Christ.

    The Samaritan woman's response was one of acceptance and belief in what the Lord Jesus Christ said, as seen in John 4:15, quote, *"The woman said to Him, Lord give me this water, in order that I thirst not nor come here to draw."* Unquote. She did not use her natural(soulish) mind to reason. If she did, she would have rejected what the Lord Jesus Christ said. Because how can any natural water quench thirst forever? She believed that Jesus could give her a type of water that could quench her thirst forever; even though she does not understand about everlasting life.

While the Jewish crowd's response in John chapter 6 to the Lord Jesus Christ was one of disbelief and rejection of what the Lord Jesus Christ claimed. They used their natural(carnal) mind to rationalize; hence they concluded with the question: How can they eat the flesh and drink the blood of Jesus Christ?

Another similar type of incident in which the Lord Jesus Christ could not make another Jew understand is John 3:1-10, where Nicodemus, the teacher of Israel, a Pharisee and a member of the Sanhedrin came to Jesus at night and acknowledged to the Lord that He believed Jesus was sent by <u>the God</u>.   Jesus, in reply told Nicodemus that if one is not born from above, he is not able to see the kingdom of <u>the God</u>. Here, we see the response of Nicodemus was between the rejection of the Jewish crowd(John 6:52) and the acceptance by the Samaritan woman(John 4:15).   Nicodemus wanted to believe the Lord Jesus Christ but when he used his natural(carnal) mind to reason he could not make out how he being old can enter into his mother's womb a second time and be born again.   The Lord Jesus Christ told Nicodemus how he not only can see the kingdom of <u>the God (John 3:3)</u>; but also how Nicodemus can enter into the kingdom of <u>the God</u>, that is how Nicodemus can receive everlasting life, by being born originating from water and Spirit(John 3:5).   The Lord Jesus Christ then went on to tell Nicodemus that the one born originating from flesh is flesh and the one born originating from the Spirit is spirit.

Let us look at the 3 cases:-

First – In the situation of the Samaritan woman, she accepted what the Lord Jesus Christ told her even though she did not understand fully what He meant. Then she asked the Lord Jesus Christ for the water which the Lord said He would give.
What was the Lord's answer?
The Lord Jesus did not give her the water to drink so that she would never thirst again; nor did the Lord Jesus Christ told her that she need not go back to the well to draw water again. Why did the Lord Jesus Christ not give the Samaritan woman what He said He would do if she ask? She did ask, but He did not give her the water. WHY? Because the water the Lord Jesus Christ talked about is the Holy Spirit. At that point in time, the Lord Jesus Christ could not give her the water(Holy Spirit) yet, because Jesus was not yet glorified (John 7:39). The Lord Jesus Christ could not explain to her when she could receive the water He promised her because He knew she could not understand spiritual matters and would be confused; that was why the Lord Jesus having known she believed Him asked her to call her husband to come, that He may also preach the good news to him.

Second – In the case of Nicodemus, he believed Jesus Christ was sent by the God; but he could not understand when the Lord Jesus Christ told him how to see and how to enter into the kingdom of the God; even though he(Nicodemus) was the teacher of Israel. What the Lord was showing Nicodemus was that even though Nicodemus was the teacher of Israel; he could not see(meaning understand) the kingdom of the God nor could he enter into the kingdom of the God, unless Nicodemus was born originating from water and Spirit. Finally, the Lord Jesus Christ told Nicodemus plainly how he could inherit everlasting life in John 3:12-21: that He is the Son of the God and that the world might be saved through Him. Only those who believe into Him will not perish but will have everlasting life. This means those who believe into Him will be born originating from water and Spirit. Then He told Nicodemus that He is the Light that has come into the world; but mankind are fond of the darkness more than the Light, because their works are evil. Because all practicing wickedness hate the Light and do not come to the Light(Jesus) so that their works may not be exposed. Only those practicing the truth(meaning the word of the God) come to Him, so that their works may be revealed having been worked in the God(John 3:21). This verse indicated that Nicodemus wanted to walk in the truth; that was why he came to see the Lord Jesus Christ and the God will work in him, meaning the God will lead him by the Spirit to do the work of the God, which are good works.

Third – In the case of the Jewish crowd in John chapter 6, they were only interested in satisfying their flesh. They only wanted Jesus to perform miracles that their flesh might be satisfied. When the Lord Jesus Christ spoke of the divine purpose of the God, they rejected Him outright. Hence their response in John 6:52.

If they had accepted what the Lord Jesus Christ said and then go on to ask Him for His flesh to eat and His blood to drink, would Jesus give them His flesh to eat and His blood to drink? Surely not! That was not what the

Lord Jesus Christ meant in the natural(carnal) sense, just as He told the Samaritan woman that He would give her water to drink that she would never thirst anymore. The Lord Jesus Christ did not give her the water as meant in the natural(fleshly) sense. He meant the Holy Spirit.

Because the Jewish crowd had tasted the food the Lord Jesus Christ had fed them, and they were satisfied(John 6:11, 26), they wanted more. The Lord Jesus Christ was not going to satisfy their flesh again. He did not come to do that, but to give them everlasting life.

Because of <u>the God</u>'s love for them, <u>the God</u> speaking through His Son continued to speak to the Jewish crowd in the terms they could understand. Instead of asking them to <u>believe into Him</u>, which He spoke 6 times(John 6:29, 30, 35, 36, 40, 47); Jesus now spoke in terms of eating and drinking(John 6:52, 53, 54, 55, 56, 57, 58). He said, quote, *"... If not you eat the flesh of the Son of the man, and drink His blood, you do not have life("zoe") in yourselves."(John 6:53).* Unquote. What is that life("zoe")? That life("zoe") is the Holy Spirit(Romans 8:10).

All mankind are dead as far as <u>the God</u> is concerned. Unless one believes into Jesus Christ one will not be born again or born originating from the Spirit. This is what John 6:53 means.

"The one chewing My flesh and drinking My blood has everlasting life("zoe") and I will raise him up the last day."(John 6:54) Unquote. John 6:54 means the same thing as John 6:40(*... everyone seeing the Son and*

believing into Him shall have everlasting life("zoe"); and I will raise him up the last day.) This also means the same thing as the Lord Jesus Christ spoke to Nicodemus in John 3:5 (*Truly, truly I say to you, if not anyone is born originating from water and Spirit, he is not able to enter into the kingdom of <u>the God</u>.)*
John 6:55 – *"For My flesh is truly food and My blood is truly drink."* What does this verse mean according to Scripture? This verse has reference in John 6:27-29.
John 6:27 - "
Do not labour(or toil) for the food which perishes, but for the food enduring to everlasting life, which the Son of the man will give to you; for <u>the God</u> stamped with a signet for preservation this One."
This verse has reference in John 4;13-14, *"Jesus answered and said to her. Everyone drinking from this, the water will thirst again; but whoever may drink from the water which I will give him, will not ever thirst forever. But the water which I will give to him will become a fountain of water in him, springing up into everlasting life."*

    The Lord Jesus Christ is the only One, <u>the God</u> has stamped with a signet for preservation who can give anyone the food or the drink that will endure or spring up to everlasting life. That food that will endure or spring up to everlasting life is the Holy Spirit and the commandments of <u>the God</u>. Only the Lord Jesus Christ is given the authority by <u>the God</u> to do this, that is to give the Holy Spirit to dwell in those <u>the God</u> called to <u>believe into Jesus Christ</u>; and He is the One who will direct them to walk in righteousness or into all the truth(John 16:13).

Thus the Lord Jesus Christ told the Jewish crowd in John 6:27, what they should do that they might do the works of <u>the God</u>. They knew that Jesus in John 6:27 talked about everlasting life. And they knew that only <u>the God</u> could give them everlasting life. So they asked what works of <u>the God</u> they must toil(or labour) in order for them to have everlasting life. The Lord's answer was given in John 6:29, quote, *This is the work of <u>the God</u>, in order that you believe into Whom that One sent."* Unquote. Therefore, John 6:55 means Jesus is the true food that will yield everlasting life. Those who <u>believe into Him</u>, He will give them the Holy Spirit who represents Christ (John 14:26), and who will lead them to obey all the truth(John 16:13), so that they can receive everlasting life.

So how can the Lord Jesus Christ give the food that will endure to everlasting life. We know in the New Testament it means Jesus Christ must die, which He did on the cross; that the body of His flesh was crucified and He poured out His blood(meaning giving up His soul life) for all mankind. And everyone who <u>believes into Him</u> is also crucified with Him on the cross and died and buried with Him that the one who died with Him will also be resurrected with Him to live forever. So the eating of His flesh and the drinking of His blood means the true believer(flesh) is also crucified with Him on the cross and gives up his soul life, that is no longer living, but the Christ lives in him. Thus, <u>believing into Him</u> is the same as eating His flesh and drinking His blood, meaning crucified and died with Him on the cross. This is confirmed in John 6:56, quote, *"The one chewing My flesh and drinking My blood remains in Me and I in him."* - meaning the one <u>believing into Jesus Christ</u> remains in the Lord Jesus Christ and the Lord remains in him.

The meaning of remaining or abiding in Jesus is also explained in John 15:4-10. To remain in Jesus Christ is the same as to remain in His word, is the same as to remain in His love, is the same as to keep or obey His commandments.

And only those who remain in Him or remain in His word are truly His disciples and they will know the truth and the truth will set them free from slavery to the sin(John 8:31-36). To be set free from slavery to the sin was also explained in Romans 6:1-6. One can only be set free from slavery to the sin if one is crucified with Christ on the cross and died and buried with Him, that is the old man/old creation/flesh died.

John 6:57 goes on to explain the meaning of remaining or abiding in Jesus Christ, quote, *"Just as the living Father sent Me, and I live through the Father, also the one chewing Me, likewise that one will live through Me."* Unquote. Jesus said that He lives through the Father – it means Jesus manifests the Father. Jesus never said or did anything on His own; everything He said and did was what the Father said and did. That was how Jesus manifested His Father. That is how Jesus lives through His Father. Jesus was 100% led by the Spirit(John 14:8, 9, 10). Therefore, true disciples are those who live through Jesus Christ – meaning the believers no longer live, but Christ lives in them. The believers do not exercise their desire/will(or walk according to flesh or self) but the believers are being led by the Spirit of the Christ or the believers do not walk according to flesh or self but walk according to the Spirit of the Christ.

   John 6:57 & 58 again emphasized that the one chewing Him lives through Him and will live forever(or have everlasting life). The believer who no longer live(died with Christ on the cross) but allows the Lord Jesus Christ to live in him by His Spirit and the believer lives through the Lord Jesus Christ, by being led by the Holy Spirit and will live forever; because it is the Spirit who gives life("zoe"), the flesh profits nothing (John 6:63). The Holy Spirit living in every true believer, is the One who represents the Lord Jesus Christ(John 14:26).

   The word "eat" appeared in all English translations of the original Greek Text – from John 6:26-58, occurring 13 times. There are 2 separate Greek words that were interpreted and translated as "eat" in John 6:26 to John 6:58. The two Greek words are: "phago" and "trogo." Nine times the Greek word "phago" appeared in verse 26(once), verse 31(twice), verse 49(once), verse 50(once), verse 51(once), verse 53(once) and verse 58(once) and all are interpreted or translated as "eat." The word "phago" means to eat(as literal and figurative).

   Four times the Greek word "trogo" appeared in verse 54(once), verse 56(once), verse 57(once) and verse 58(once) and all are interpreted or translated as "eat." The word "trogo" has the meaning of corrosion or wear; or to gnaw or chew, that is a type of eating.
   However, almost all bible translators simply used the word "eat" as meaning for "phago" and also for "trogo."

Why did the Lord Jesus Christ use two different Greek words "phago" and "trogo" to describe eating? Scriptures itself give the reason for using the two different words "phago" and "trogo" to mean different type of eating. John 6:58, quote, *"This is the Bread which comes down originating from the heaven, not in the manner as your fathers ate("phago") the manna, and died. The one chewing("trogo") from this Bread will live forever."* Unquote. "Phago" refers to just eating; while "trogo" refers to more than normal eating; it means gnawing or chewing. To receive everlasting life("zoe") the Lord Jesus Christ used the word "trogo", to reveal that the believer must gnaw or chew the Bread – this means the believing must be stronger and stronger(that is increasing faith) until the believer is 100% led by the Spirit and 0% led by the self.

    To confirm what the Lord Jesus Christ said about eating and chewing His flesh and drinking His blood means <u>believing into Him</u>, the Lord Jesus Christ in John 6:63 said, *"It is the Spirit who makes alive, the flesh does not profit, nothing! The words which I speak to you are Spirit and are Life("zoe").*

    This means the words that the Lord Jesus Christ speaks are Spirit and are Life("zoe"); so whatever word the Lord Jesus speaks are spiritual and not fleshly or of the flesh. Thus when the Lord Jesus Christ talked about drinking water, He did not mean natural water or anything physical; He meant the Holy Spirit(John 4:14). When the Lord Jesus told the Jewish crowd not to labor for food that perishes but to labor for food enduring to everlasting life; and He is the One who will give the food enduring to everlasting life; the food He talked about is the Holy Spirit and the commandments of the God(John 6:27). The Lord Jesus Christ will give to those who **believe into Him** the food (Holy Spirit and the commandments of the God) enduring to everlasting life after He had done the will of His Father, that is to pay the penalty for all mankind's sins and took away the sin of the world; then He(Jesus) would be resurrected and given everlasting life and return to His Father in the heaven. And the Father would give Him the promise of the Holy Spirit(John 7:39 & Acts 2:33). So when Jesus said that His flesh is truly food and His blood is truly drink (John 6:55) He meant that as a man(flesh) He had to give up His soul(the soul is in the blood – Leviticus 17:11) so that the Father will give the promised Holy Spirit to Him and He can then pour the Holy Spirit upon all those who **believe into Him** that they may have everlasting life. Therefore to eat His flesh and to drink His blood is to **believe into Him**, and that is to obey the gospel or to obey the Lord Jesus Christ.

    In John 6:64, the Lord Jesus Christ talked about **believing** again, quote, *"But there are from you some who are not **believing**!"* For the Lord Jesus Christ knew from the beginning who they are, the ones **not believing**, and who is the one who is about to betray Him.

    Then in John 6:59, Simon Peter answered the Lord, *"And we **believe** and have known that You are the Christ, the Son of the living God."* Peter understood that chewing His flesh and drinking His blood means **believing into Him**. Peter did not say, "Yes Lord, we know that unless we chew Your flesh and drink Your blood we would not have everlasting life." Instead, Peter said, *"We **believed** and have known that You are the Christ, the Son of the living God."*

Many who misinterpreted the Lord's comments of "Eating My flesh and drinking My blood" as part of the Lord's table, also have the misconception that wine has to be used in partaking the Lord's table because alcohol passes unchanged directly into our bloodstream, thus Jesus' life blood flows through the believers' veins and that is how the believers have the life of Jesus Christ which becomes everlasting life in the believers.

Comments:- Leviticus 17:11, quote, *"Because the soul of the flesh is in the blood; and I have given it to you upon the altar to make atonement for your souls. Because it is the blood that makes atonement for the soul."* Unquote.

Man was created a living soul(Genesis 2:7; 1 Corinthians 15:45). A man's soul is in his blood. Jesus Christ came as a man(flesh), a living soul; therefore His soul is in His blood – that is true. When Jesus Christ died on the cross, He gave up His soul on behalf of all mankind. The words "shed blood" means "giving up the soul." But the God raised Jesus Christ up from the dead to become a New Man(New Creation), a Spiritual Man, with a spiritual body(1 Corinthians 15:44, 45). When Jesus was on the earth the first time, He came as an Adamic man, that is a living soul. In fact He came as the last Adam. Now, as the Resurrected Christ, He is a Spiritual Man, alive in Spirit, not a soulish(natural) man like Adam(or any mankind on the earth) anymore. Jesus had been converted from natural man(living soul) to being made alive in Spirit. He has a spiritual body or flesh that has no blood. Only natural man(living soul) has blood.

When true believers died with Him on the cross, it means the old man(flesh or soul) died – meaning the believers do not exercise their will/desires anymore. The Resurrected Christ then lives in the true believers by His Spirit in the hearts of the true believers(not the physical heart). To say when believers drink the wine they receive Jesus life blood flowing through their veins, means that the believers receive not the new creation(Resurrected Christ) but the old creation, the last Adam, His soul into the believers' blood. This means the believers go back to the old creation – the Adamic race. But Jesus who came as the last Adam died and gave up His soul and <u>the God</u> raised Him up not as a living soul or Adamic man, but as the New Creation, the Spiritual Man to live forever (1 Corinthians 15:44-45; 1 Peter 3:18).

Scriptures say that those who are in Christ Jesus are a new creation(2 Corinthians 5:17; Galatians 6:15). This means the Spirit of Christ(the Resurrected Christ) lives in the true believers and not the soul of the last Adam living in the believers. Scriptures also say that flesh and blood cannot inherit the kingdom of God(1 Corinthians 15:50), meaning the old creation, that is the living soul cannot inherit the kingdom of God. It is therefore ridiculous to suggest that by drinking wine(partaking the Lord's table), the life blood of Jesus flows through the veins of the partaker, thereby giving everlasting life. The Resurrected Christ by His Spirit does not give a believer another soul(life - "psuche"), but Himself is the everlasting life("zoe") living in the believers, but not in the blood stream of the believers. That is why in the New Testament two Greek words for life are used: "psuche", which means soul – which is in all Adamic mankind and "zoe" meaning life as in life everlasting – the new life or new creation. Jesus Christ Himself gave up His soul("psuche") to receive everlasting life("zoe"). Those believers who do not give up their lives("psuche" - souls) on behalf of the Lord Jesus Christ will not receive everlasting life("zoe") from the Lord (Matthew 10:39; Matthew 16:25; Mark 8:35; Luke 9:24; Luke 17:33 & John 12:25).

So the idea or rationalization of human intellect that "alcohol passes unchanged, directly into the blood stream of the believers; thus Jesus life blood flows through the veins of the believers – would mean Jesus, the old creation(flesh), the last Adam lives in the believers and gives them life("psuche" -soul). Remember, Jesus said, "flesh gives birth to flesh and Spirit gives birth to spirit"(John 3:6). It is the Resurrected Christ, in Spirit who lives in true believers and it would not be in the blood, because the life("psuche" - soul), old creation is in the blood.

It has been shown that John 6:41-66 is not related to the Lord's table as spoken by Paul in 1 Corinthians 11:23-26. There is no confirmation in the 4 gospels of Matthew, Mark, Luke and John that the cup that Jesus shared with His 12 apostles was wine. Let us look at the specific scriptures:-

Matthew 26:26-29
1) v29 – But I say to you that not ever will I drink from this offspring(or fruit or produce - "gennema") of the vine until that day when I drink it new with you in the kingdom of My Father.

2) Mark 14:22-25
v25 – Truly, I say to you that no longer, not ever I may drink from the offspring(or fruit or produce - "gennema") of the vine until that day when I drink it new in the kingdom of <u>the God</u>."

3) Luke 22:17-20
v18 – for I say to you that not ever will I drink from the offspring(or fruit or produce - "gennema") of the vine until when the kingdom of <u>the God</u> comes.

The Greek word for "wine" is "oinos" and this word "oinos" is not used in the scriptures relating to the Lord's table. The word used by the Lord Jesus Christ is "gennema" meaning offspring or produce.

The fact that the Lord did not use the word "oinos" to specify wine, but instead used the word "gennema" meaning offspring or produce meant it is not essential that the cup must contain wine. They might actually be using wine for the occasion but since it was not specifically mentioned and the word offspring or produce was specifically mentioned by the Lord Jesus Christ would tell us this:- whether the drink in the cup is wine or something else is not the essential point. The essential point is that they shared the cup together. If wine is the essence, then the Lord would certainly use the word "oinos."

In 1 Corinthians 11:23-26, Paul taught the Corinth believers how to partake the Lord's table. Paul did not say what was in the cup.

In 1 Corinthians 11:21, Paul admonished the Corinth believers for eating to fill their hunger and also drinking to get drunk in the gathering of the church. This is improper and not the aim of the Lord's table. They should eat their meal in their homes. The Lord's table is not to satisfy the need of the flesh, but has a spiritual significance which the Corinth believers misused. So verse 21 did not specifically mention that the cup they were partaking was wine. Even if it was wine, it was not the essence, because if wine is the essence Paul or the Lord Jesus Christ would have mentioned it specifically and not indirectly.

The true meaning or spiritual significance of the Lord's table is explained by Paul in 1 Corinthians 10:16 & 17. The mechanics or ways of partaking the Lord's table is given in 1 Corinthians 11:23-26.

The correct translation of 1 Corinthians 10:16 & 17 is this:-
v16 – The cup of the blessing which we bless, is it not a partnership of the blood of the Christ? The bread which we break, is it not a partnership of the body of the Christ?
v17 – because we, the many are one bread, one body, for we all partake from the one bread.

In the partaking of the Lord's table, all true believers are making a declaration individually and collectively that they are in partnership with the Lord Jesus Christ in the likeness of His suffering (His body being broken for His disciples) and even until the likeness of His death. The Lord Jesus Christ suffered at the hands of evil men because He walked righteously according to the will of the Father, the God. So, in partaking the Lord's table believers also declare that *they* are walking righteously in partnership with the Lord Jesus Christ and being led by the Lord Jesus in suffering and even until death. The type of sufferings and death for each believer is to be decided by the Lord Jesus Christ Himself. All believers are to accept willingly. This is the true meaning of partaking the Lord's table.

    Also in the partaking of the Lord's table, believers must realize that the body of the Lord Jesus Christ is the true holy temple of the God(John 2:19, 21). Each believer is not only allowed to be in the temple but also be a part of the temple of the God, as collectively believers are the body of the Christ. Therefore, as believers coming to partake the Lord's table, individually and collectively they must ensure that they have kept their bodies holy. All unconfessed sins must first be repented before coming to the Lord's table. And it is also the duty of individuals and collectively as a body to ensure that no unbelievers are allowed to be part of the Lord's table; so that the body is not defiled. This is the true meaning of partaking the Lord's table, other than to thank the Lord and also to remember His great sacrifice for all the believers.

CONCLUSION

    "Eating My flesh and drinking My blood" means "believing into the Lord Jesus Christ", the end result is everlasting life.

- END -

BOOKLET THREE

THE LORD JESUS CHRIST WASHING THE FEET OF HIS TWELVE APOSTLES
(John 13:4-17)

INTRODUCTION

There are some "Christian groups" who continue to practice the literal washing of each other's feet on a regular basis following what the Lord Jesus Christ told His apostles in John 13:4-17. Is this practice according to the command of the Lord Jesus Christ?

This booklet is released to reveal the truth concerning the commandment by the Lord Jesus Christ to His apostles who are also disciples to wash each other's feet – what is the true meaning of washing each other's feet.

WHAT IS THE SIGNIFICANCE?

John 13:4-17
v4 *– He rises from the dinner and sets aside the garments and taking a towel and girds tightly Himself.*
v5 *– Then He puts water into the basin and begins to wash the feet of the disciples, and to wipe dry with the towel which He girded tightly.*
v6 *- Accordingly, He comes toward Simon Peter. And that one says to Him, Lord, You wash my feet?*

v7 – *Jesus answered and said to him, What I am doing, you do not know yet. But you will know after these things.*
v8 – *Peter said to Him, Not ever You cleanse my feet into the ages. Jesus answered him, If not I wash you, you have no part with Me.*
v9 – *Simon Peter said to him, Lord not only my feet, but also the hands and the head.*
v10 – *Jesus said to him, The one having been bathed has no requirement than to wash the feet.*
v11 – *For He knew the one betraying Him. Through this He said, Not all are clean.*
v12 – *Accordingly, then He washed their feet and having taken His garments, reclined again. He said to them, Do you know what I have done?*
v13 – *You called Me the Teacher and the Lord, and you say well, for I am.*
v14 – *Accordingly, if I washed your feet, the Lord and the Teacher, you also ought to wash the feet of one another.*
v15 – *For I gave a pattern to you, in order that just as I did to you, you should also do.*
v16 – *Truly, truly I say to you, a slave is not greater than his lord, nor a messenger greater than the one sending him.*
v17 – *If you know these things, you are blessed if you do them.*

What is the message that the Lord Jesus Christ wanted to teach His apostles in the incident of washing His disciples' feet with water?

   At the time when the Lord Jesus Christ washed the feet of His twelve disciples, they did not understand the significance of what He was doing to them. But the Lord Jesus Christ told them afterwards that they would know (John 13:7-8).

   When at first Peter would not allow the Lord Jesus Christ to wash his feet, because in his humanistic(flesh or old creation) thinking, "how can he allow His master to do the job of a slave?" Peter was thinking well of the Lord Jesus Christ in the humanistic way. The Lord Jesus' answer to Peter seemed harsh according to the humanistic way, quote, *"If not I wash you, you have no part with Me."* unquote. What Peter in his humanistic(fleshly) way of not allowing the Lord Jesus Christ, his Master to do such a degrading job, that is to wash his feet, was in fact opposing the way of the God! That was why the Lord Jesus Christ's answer to Peter appeared to be harsh in the humanistic thinking. But the Lord Jesus Christ was telling Peter the truth! Unless Peter allowed the Lord Jesus Christ to wash his(Peter) feet, Peter would not be part of the Lord's overall plan of salvation for the called out ones.

   The reaction of Peter in John 13:7-8 is typical of how human(flesh or old creation) would react for the "good" of the other person(flesh or mankind), just as Peter told the Lord Jesus Christ in Matthew 16:22 and the Lord Jesus' "harsh" answer to Peter in Matthew 16:23-25. In Matthew 16:21 the Lord Jesus Christ told His disciples that He had

to suffer many things from the elders and chief priests and scribes and to be killed and later raised up on the third day. Peter began to rebuke the Lord Jesus Christ by saying that *"that should never happen to the Lord."* Peter in his humanistic thinking, being motivated by Satan showed his concern for the Lord Jesus Christ as a man, not wanting the Lord Jesus Christ to suffer persecution and death at the hands of the elders, chief priests and scribes. In normal humanistic terms this is "good thinking and showing care" by Peter who was sincere in his thinking and care for the Lord Jesus Christ. But in the eyes of the God, Peter was doing the bidding of Satan, trying to thwart the will of the God or the plan of the God for the salvation of those mankind the God had/has/will have called. That was why the Lord's answer to Peter appeared harsh, quote, *"Go behind Me, Satan!"* unquote. The Lord Jesus Christ also gave the reason why Peter's answer to Him in Matthew 16:22 was in opposition to the plan of the
God, quote, *"You are an offence to Me because you do not think of the things of the God, but the things of the mankind."* (Matthew 16:23), unquote.

    The thinking and action of Peter in Matthew 16:22 and John 13:7-8 are so relevant in all mankind of the past and even of today. All mankind including the apostles and disciples of Christ if they think according to their own will/desire what are good for other mankind or even for the Lord Jesus Christ – their thinking and intention will always be in opposition to the thinking/inclination and will of the God.
    WHY?

Paul explained this in Romans 8:5-8. All mankind who show concern according to their own (flesh, old creation, human) thinking only care for the things of flesh(or mankind) but those mankind who show concern according to the thinking/inclination/will of the Spirit are caring for the things of the Spirit, which are the things of the God. The thinking/inclination/will of the flesh (human, old creation) is death but the thinking/inclination/will of the Spirit is life and peace. Because the thinking/inclination/will of the flesh(mankind) is enmity toward God and can never please God. No matter who you are and how learned you are in the word of the God, what position you hold in any so-called "Christian organization", if you care according to flesh(human, old creation) and not according to Spirit, you will always oppose the ways of the God and you become an enemy of the God.

Peter's concern in Matthew 16:22 and John 13:7-8 for the Lord Jesus Christ was based on his own(humanistic, fleshly, old creation) thinking of "care and good" for the Lord Jesus Christ. Because all mankind descended from Adam are from the corrupt tree, all mankind are no good; in fact all mankind are evil, because the sin is in all mankind, passed down from Adam and Eve. The sin is also the lawlessness. (Genesis 6:5; Genesis 8:21; Matthew 7:11; Matthew 12:34; Luke 11:13; Romans 5:12; 1 John 3:4). Since all mankind are evil it means that the heart of all mankind are evil as revealed by the Lord Jesus Christ in Matthew 7:11; Matthew 12:34 and Luke 11:13.

A corrupt tree can never produce good fruits, but a corrupt tree always produce evil fruits (Matthew 7:17-20). The thinking/inclination/will of mankind are from the heart; and if the heart is evil then every thinking/inclination/will of mankind are evil. No good can come out of evil mankind's thinking/inclination/will. In fact every thought and intention of mankind's heart is confined to evil continually according to Genesis 6:5. What mankind want to do good will end up doing evil, just as Paul revealed about himself in Romans 7:14-24. Paul knew the law and commandments are good, holy and righteous and Paul wanted to do good, meaning he wanted to obey/keep/follow the law and commandments of the God, but as he revealed in Romans 7:14-24, he ended up doing evil, meaning that he ended up breaking the law and commandments of the God.

    Many so-called Christians who read the texts of Matthew 16:21-23 and John 13:4-17 tend to laugh at Peter. Peter's ways in Matthew 16:21-23 and John 13:7-8 personify the ways of all mankind(old creation). We (mankind, flesh, old creation) who laugh at Peter are only laughing at our own selves. All mankind(believers or unbelievers, Jews or Greeks) without exception when they use their own minds to plan and to do "good" will always end up "doing evil." This is the teaching of the Lord Jesus Christ and Paul. The teaching of the Lord Jesus Christ are not His own but from His Father, the God(John 7:16-17). Paul was taught by the Lord Jesus Christ directly through His Spirit.

What then is the significance of the washing of the feet of the disciples by the Lord and Teacher – Jesus Christ?

When Peter at first would not allow the Lord Jesus Christ to wash his feet and was told by the Lord Jesus Christ that unless the Lord wash his feet, Peter would have no part with the Lord Jesus Christ; Peter, then in his humanistic thinking that he would want to be part of the plan of the God, told the Lord that not just to wash his feet, but he also wanted the Lord to wash his hands and head as well. Again this shows that with our humanistic (fleshly) mind, if we try to draw conclusion other than what the Lord Jesus Christ had also clearly stated, we would again and again be wrong.

The Lord Jesus Christ then answered Peter that the one who had been bathed had no need to wash again except to wash his feet, because he was already clean. If his feet was washed, he would be wholly clean.

The Lord Jesus' physical act of washing His disciples' feet with water and cleaning them with a towel is His demonstration of the word of the God in human terms. The word of the God is spiritual, because the God is Spirit (Romans 7:14; John 4:24). All mankind are flesh and therefore fleshly. The fleshly can never understand the spiritual. All the disciples of the Lord Jesus Christ during the time when the Lord Jesus Christ was still alive and on the earth, were fleshly, meaning they were not spiritual – because with the exception of the Lord Jesus Christ, no mankind or flesh has the indwelling of the Holy Spirit, not even the twelve apostles because Jesus Christ has not been glorified to the right of His Father in heaven. Therefore the Holy Spirit cannot be given yet (John 7:37-39; Acts 2:33; John 14:26; John 16:7-15). Only when the apostles received the Holy Spirit were they able to understand all the teaching of the Lord Jesus Christ. Paul also revealed that only the spiritual can understand the word of the God when he rebuked the fleshly Corinth believers in 1 Corinthians 2:13-16; 1 Corinthians 3:1-3.

The Lord Jesus Christ in John 13:4-17 was using a fleshly act to show the spiritual meaning of the word of the God.

All the disciples whom the God called and sent to His Son(John 6:39-40, 44-45) will come to Jesus Christ who is the One who will give them food enduring to everlasting life(John 6:27). When those who come to Jesus Christ, their sins will be forgiven and they are cleansed from all unrighteousness. But because those called are still on the earth and *the sin* is still in them, they will continually fall into walking according to flesh or thinking according to flesh(self) and will end up doing works in opposition to the commands and law of the God and this is considered as evil or sin and had to be cleansed again. Those who are called by the God to salvation and when the respond affirmatively by going to the Lord Jesus Christ, all their sins will be cleansed and forgiven. However, believers still have the sin in them(flesh) and they have to continuously declared themselves dead to the sin or dead to the self or they must continuously deny utterly selves and bear their crosses of death to follow the Lord Jesus Christ, who is represented living in believers by the Holy Spirit. Therefore believers must 100% sow, walk and live according to Spirit and must not at all sow, walk and live according to flesh(self), otherwise they will fall into sin again. This is of course impossible for any flesh who has become a believer to attain – that is to be 100% led by the Spirit of Christ to follow/keep/obey the commands of the Lord Jesus Christ at all times. This means believers who are still in flesh will every so often fall back to walking and living according to flesh(self). And because *the sin* is still in the flesh of every mankind, whenever the believer walks and lives according to flesh, he will sin against the God and requires forgiveness. This is done through repentance, meaning for the believer to turn back to the Lord Jesus Christ and continue to walk and live according to Spirit. What does it mean for believers to turn back to the Lord Jesus Christ? It means the believers must turn to follow the word of the Lord Jesus Christ which are the word and commands of the God. In this way the believers are being sanctified by the word of the God which is *the truth*(John 17:17). Jesus Christ is the personification of the *word of the God* (Revelation 19:13), because He is 100% obedient to all the commandments and word of the God – therefore Jesus Christ is *the truth*(John 14:6) – *the word of the God*. All believers are sanctified or cleansed by the Lord Jesus Christ who leads all the true believers to keep/follow/obey the word of the God through the Holy Spirit(John 16:13).

Water represents the *word of the God*. Those who keep/follow/obey the *word of the God* or who keep/obey/follow the Lord Jesus Christ are being cleansed or sanctified(John 17:17).

All those the God called to salvation are called out of the world and they are no more of the world, meaning they do not belong to the world, but because they are still in flesh, they are still living in the world. To be no more of the world means to be no more conforming to the ways of the world, which means to be no more living as flesh or old creation. The world means the ways of the flesh or ways of the old creation. To be called out of the world is not a once off affair or process. It takes a long process to lead mankind out of their old ways or their own thinking/desire to follow the ways and thinking/desire of the God, who is represented by the Lord Jesus Christ through the Holy Spirit living in the heart of all true believers. The Lord Jesus Christ is now sitting at the right of the God, His Father in heaven, He is represented by the Holy Spirit living in the heart of all true believers.

The feet of the followers of the Lord Jesus Christ represent the contact of the followers with the world. As long as followers are in contact with the word because they are still in the world, they will tend go back to the ways and thinking of the world. The world or the old creation or flesh have their standards of what is good and care. And the standards of flesh or old creation tend to change with time. But the true standard of what is good and care is the God, whose definition of what is good never changes, meaning the ways of the God never change.

Followers of the Lord Jesus Christ are constantly convicted by the Holy Spirit living in them to repent when they fall back to following the ways of the world. Followers of Christ must constantly look to the Lord Jesus Christ for the ways and standard to follow.

Whenever followers of Christ fall back to their old ways or fleshly ways of thinking or the ways of the world their feet are dirty and need to be cleansed. This means when followers of Christ fall away from following the Lord Jesus Christ, they fail to listen to the voice of the Holy Spirit and as time goes by they become unable to hear the voice of the Holy Spirit. *Then how do they know that their feet are corrupted or that they need to be cleansed from unrighteousness?*

This is the reason for the example shown by the Lord Jesus Christ in the washing of the feet of His disciples and His command to the disciples to wash each other's feet. The Lord Jesus Christ is the One who cleanses His disciples of their sins when they fall away from Him by admonishing them of their fleshly ways which are evil ways to turn them from their evil ways to return to follow the righteous ways of the Lord Jesus Christ by reminding them of the word and commands of the God which are also the word and commands of the Lord Jesus Christ. The commands and word of the Lord Jesus Christ are symbolized by water. When the followers who fall away from the Lord return to follow/keep/obey the commands and word of the Lord Jesus Christ they are being cleansed or sanctified by the word of the God. Disciples of the

Lord Jesus Christ are to follow His example – they are to wash each other's feet – meaning they are to admonish each other with *the truth* which is *the word of the God* so that if any disciples fall into sin they can turn back to follow the Lord Jesus Christ and be cleansed from all unrighteousness. **Whatever sins that have been forgiven or cleansed need not be forgiven or cleansed again.**

That was why Paul having turned to the Lord Jesus Christ in repentance, need not have to ask the Lord Jesus Christ for forgiveness again for his part in the persecution of the church.

Throughout the epistles of Paul, Peter, James and John are many incidences of teaching and admonishment of the followers of Christ to turn back from their sins to follow the Lord Jesus Christ again. What Paul, Peter, James and John wrote and did in their epistles are examples of their following the example of the Lord Jesus Christ of washing each other's feet(John 13:4-17). There is no record of anyone performing the same physical act of washing the feet of other disciples in water. WHY? Because this is not what the Lord required to be done – the physical act of washing each other's feet.

Water represents the Word of the God as revealed in Ephesians 5:26.

- END -

BOOKLET FOUR

THE NON-LITERAL MEANING OF WATER IN THE NEW TESTAMENT SCRIPTURES

In the New Testament Scriptures, other than its literal meaning, water("hundar") is also taken to mean:-

[1] Cleansing or purifying one from uncleanliness or from uncleanliness of sins as seen in the following scriptures:-

\# Matthew 27:24
\# Luke 7:44
\# John 13:5
\# Matthew 3:11; Mark 1:8; Luke 13:16; John 1:26; John 1:31, 33; John 3:23
\# Acts 1:5; Acts 11:16

The water baptism conducted by John the Baptist on those who believed in John's message of turning away from unrighteousness to following the ways of righteousness by showing fruit worthy of the repentance – has the meaning of washing or cleaning the one being baptized in water from old ways of unrighteousness or that he can follow the ways of righteousness.

[2] The putting to death of the flesh or old creation or self and to follow the God in the following scriptures:-

\#   Matthew 3:16
\#   Mark 1:9-10
\#   John 1:33

    The baptism of Jesus Christ in water by John the Baptist is not the same or does not have the same meaning as the water baptism conducted by John the Baptist on Jews who believed John's message of following the ways of righteousness.
    Those Jews who came to John the Baptist to be baptized in water came to make a commitment that as they were immersed in water by John the Baptist, they are turning over from their old ways of walking and living in unrighteousness to follow the way of righteousness (Matthew 21:31). That is called baptism of repentance (Acts 19:1-4).

    The baptism of Jesus Christ in water by John the Baptist is not a baptism of repentance because Jesus Christ is sinless and has never sinned against the God.   That is why John the Baptist at first refused to baptize Jesus Christ. The Lord Jesus Christ told John the Baptist to baptize Him in "water" because that is the proper way *"to us"* (meaning to all who are called by the God to salvation) to *fulfil all righteousness*(Matthew 3:15).
    The water baptism that Jesus Christ as a sinless man underwent is the beginning for all New Testament believers to follow in their journey to *fulfil all righteousness*.

Jesus Christ as a man is sinless, and He has nothing to repent or turn away from. But He underwent water baptism as His starting point to fulfil the Law and the Prophets(Matthew 5:17-18). Why the need for Jesus Christ to undergo water baptism?

The moment Jesus Christ went under the water of baptism He voluntarily declared His own death or death to Self or Flesh. That is why when He rose from the water of baptism, the God sent the Holy Spirit to come upon Him and to dwell in Him in fullness, to lead Him for the rest of His life-span on the earth as a man. Because Jesus Christ from hence forth denied utterly Himself and bore His cross of death, His Father the God then gave the Holy Spirit to dwell in Jesus Christ to lead Jesus Christ to do the will of God, His Father, or to fulfil the Law and the Prophets. The Holy Spirit dwelling in Jesus Christ represents the God, the Father of Jesus Christ. From henceforth whatever Jesus Christ said and did were not from His own thought/desire/will but what the God, His Father wanted Him to say and/or to do. This was how Jesus Christ fulfilled the Law and the Prophets by being 100% obedient to the Father by being 100% led by the Holy Spirit.

Even though Jesus Christ while He was on the earth the first time was a man(John 8:40) and flesh(John 1:14) yet whatever He said and did were not from flesh(Self) but from Spirit(John 6:63).

That was why Paul in Acts 19:1-7 had to baptize again the twelve disciples of John the Baptist although they were already baptized in water by John the Baptist. Paul had to baptize them again in water in the name of the Lord

Jesus Christ – meaning they had to undergo a water baptism similar to Jesus Christ, to declare that they were dead to the self or they were to be put to death in conformity to the death of Jesus Christ on the cross (Romans 6:1-4), in order that as they were immersed in the water of baptism they declared their death with the Christ on the cross and they no longer live but the Christ lives in them through His Spirit(Romans 6:1-6; Galatians 2:20) and on arising from the water baptism, with the laying on of hands by Paul they then received the Holy Spirit who then dwelled in their hearts. The Holy Spirit representing the Lord Jesus Christ(John 14:26) is the One who would teach and lead them into all the truth(John 16:13).

Therefore water baptism in New Testament days represents putting to death of the self or flesh or the old creation and on arising from the water baptism, the believer then manifests the Lord Jesus Christ by allowing the Holy Spirit who lives in him to lead him to do the will of the Lord Jesus Christ, which is the will of the God and that is to fulfil all righteousness.

Water baptism in New Testament days is not a symbolism as popularly taught. It is a voluntary commitment by the called out one undergoing water baptism to conform to the declaration by the God that He had put all mankind to death on the cross, when the God made His Son, Jesus Christ as the last Adam(1 Corinthians 15:45) – because this is the only way the God can save those He called/being called/will call to salvation – an act declared by the God, but must be made real or fulfilled in those the God called/being called/will call to salvation, who believe(d) what He had done – and the practical reality is seen in the believers doing good works.

[3] The Holy Spirit whom the Lord Jesus Christ promised those who believe into Him will receive when He returns to His Father, the God in heaven(John 14:16-17, 26; John 15:26; John 16:7-15).

Water is also used by the Lord Jesus Christ in reference to the Holy Spirit whom the Lord Jesus Christ will petition His Father to send to dwell in His disciples. Scriptures relating water or living water to the Holy Spirit are: John 4:10-15; John 7:37-39.

The Holy Spirit can only be given to the Lord Jesus Christ's disciples when He returns to His Father, being exalted to the right of the God in heaven(John 7:37-39; Acts 2:33; Acts 1:4-5, 8).

The receiving of the Holy Spirit by the disciples of Christ is also called "baptized in Holy Spirit" as revealed by John the Baptist and the Lord Jesus Christ and Peter in Matthew 3:11; Mark 1:8; Luke 3:16; Acts 1:5; Acts 11:16.

The Holy Spirit has been referred to as water or living water because it is through the Holy Spirit that followers of the Christ will be made clean or cleansed or washed of all defilement. HOW? The Holy Spirit will convict them of their sins and will reveal or teach them the truth(or the true meaning of the word of the God) and will also lead or guide them to keep/follow/obey the truth, which is the word of the God. This way believers are purified from all defilement or perfected in holiness or sanctified in the truth(word of the God)(John 17:17). By themselves(flesh, old creation)believers are unable to understand the truth nor are they able to keep/follow/obey the truth. Only the Holy Spirit of the truth, who represents the Christ living all true believers can explain and reveal the truth to the believers and also is the One who will lead believers to keep/follow/obey the truth in order that believers be made righteous, holy and good.

[4] The word of the God or the word and utterance of Jesus Christ are also referred to as water in John 3:5; Ephesians 5:26; Hebrews 9:19; Hebrews 10:22 and 1 John 5:6, 8.

After those who have been called by the God to follow the Lord Jesus Christ(John 6:44-45, 65) have been forgiven of their sins and given the Holy Spirit(being born from the Spirit or baptized in Holy Spirit), they need to be purified from all defilements of flesh and breath of life(2 Corinthians 7:1) in order that they can be perfected in holiness in fear of God and this is done through the Lord Jesus Christ by His Spirit living in all true believers by being sanctified according to the truth which is the word of the God(John 17:17, 19). Or the Lord Jesus Christ sanctify them by the washing of the water in His words(or commandments)(Ephesians 5:26) in order that the Lord Jesus Christ might present to Himself the glorious church not having spots or wrinkle but that it be holy and without blemish(Ephesians 5:27). **That is how called out ones are saved.**

[5] Everlasting life is also referred to as water in descriptions in Revelation 21:6; Revelation 22:1, 17; John 7:37-39; John 4:10-14.

APPENDIX – SCRIPTURES IN THE NEW TESTAMENT WITH THE TRANSLATED WORD "WATER"

(1) *Matthew 27:24 – And knowing that nothing is gained, but rather an uproar happens, Pilate taking <u>water</u> he washed the hands before the crowd, saying, I am innocent from the blood of this righteous one, you see.*

(2) *Mark 9:41 – For whoever may give you a cup of <u>water</u> to drink in My name because you are of Christ, truly I say to you, No way he will lose his reward.*

(3) *Luke 7:44 – And turning toward the woman, He said to Simon, In this way, see the woman. I entered into your house, you gave Me no <u>water</u> upon My feet, but she wet My feet with tears and wiped off with the hair of her head.*

(4) *Matthew 3:11 – I indeed baptize you in <u>water</u> into repentance. But the one coming after me is stronger than Me, of whom I am not competent to lift the sandals. He will baptize you in Holy Spirit and fire.*

(5) *Mark 1:8 – I indeed baptize you in <u>water</u>, but He will baptize you in Holy Spirit.*

(6) *Luke 3:16 – John answered to everyone, saying, I indeed baptize you in <u>water</u>. But the One stronger than me of whom I am not competent to loosen the strap of His sandals. He will baptize you in Holy Spirit and fire,*

(7) *John 1:26 – John answered them saying, I baptize in <u>water</u>, but Whom stands in your midst, you know not,*

(8) *Matthew 3:16 – And being baptized Jesus went up at once from the <u>water</u>, and behold the heavens were opened to Him and He discerned the Spirit of the God descending as if a dove, and coming upon Him.*

(9) *Mark 1:9-10 – And it became in those the days, Jesus came from Nazareth of the Galilee, and was baptized by John in the Jordan. And at once going up from the <u>water</u> he discerned the heavens opened and the Spirit as if a dove coming down upon Him.*

(10) *John 1:31 – And I knew Him not, but in order that He be revealed to Israel. Through this I came baptizing in the <u>water</u>.*

(11) *John 1:33 – And I knew Him not, but the One sending me to baptize in <u>water</u>, that One said to me, Upon whomever you see the Spirit coming down and remaining upon Him, in this way is the One baptizing in Holy Spirit.*

(12) *John 3:5 – Truly, truly I say to you, If not anyone be born originating from <u>water</u> and Spirit, he is not able to enter into the kingdom of the God.*

(13) *John 3:23 – But John was also baptizing in Aenon near the Salem, because there were abundant <u>waters</u>. And they came and were baptized.*

(14) *John 4:10 – Jesus answered and said to her, If you knew the gift of the God, and who is the One saying to you, Give Me to drink, you would have asked Him, and He would give you <u>living water</u>.*

(15) John 4:13-14 – Jesus answered and said to her, Every one drinking originating from this, the <u>water</u> will thirst again. But whoever may drink originating from the <u>water</u> which I will give him, not ever will thirst into the age, but the <u>water</u> which I will give him will become in him a fountain of <u>water</u>, springing up into everlasting life.

(16) John 4:15 – The woman said toward Him, Give me this, the <u>water</u>, in order that I thirst not, nor come here to draw.

(17) John 5:3 – Lying in these was a large populace of the infirm, blind, lame, withered, awaiting the stirring of the <u>water</u>.

(18) John 5:4 – For at time an angel descended in the pool, and agitated the water. Accordingly, the one first entering after the agitation of the <u>water</u> becomes healthy, at any time whatever disease he was held down.

(19) John 7: 37-39
But in the last day of the great feast, Jesus stood and called aloud, saying, If anyone thirst, come toward Me and drink.
The one believing into Me, just as the writing said, Rivers originating from his belly will flow <u>living water</u>.
But He said this concerning the Spirit whom the ones believing into Him were about to receive. For the Spirit was not yet (given) because Jesus was not yet glorified.

(20) John 13:4 – 17

(21) *John 19:34* – *but one of the soldiers pierced His side with a lance. And immediately came out blood and <u>water</u>.*

(22) *Acts 1:5* – *because John indeed baptized in <u>water</u>, but you will be baptized in Holy Spirit in this way not many days after.*

(23) *Acts 8:36* – *And in that manner they were going according to the way, they came upon some <u>water</u>, and the eunuch said, Behold! <u>Water</u>, What prevents me to be baptized?*

(24) *Acts 8:39* – *But when they came up out of the <u>water</u>, Spirit Lord seized Philip away, and the eunuch saw him no more; for he went his way rejoicing.*

(25) *Acts 10:47* – *Whether at all anyone is able to forbid the <u>water</u> these the ones not to be baptized who have received the Holy Spirit just as we also?*

(26) *Acts 11:16* – *But I remembered the Lord's utterance, in that manner He said, John indeed baptized with <u>water</u>, but you will be baptized in Holy Spirit.*

(27) *Ephesians 5:26* – *in order that He might sanctify, cleansing by the washing of the <u>water</u> in utterance*

(28) *Hebrews 9:19* – *For having spoken every commandment according to the Law by Moses to all the people having taken the blood of the calves and goats with <u>water</u> and scarlet wool and hyssop, he sprinkled both the scroll and all the people.*

(29) Hebrews 10:22 – draw near with a true heart in full assurance of faith, having sprinkled the hearts from an evil conscience, and having washed the body with clean <u>water</u>;

(30) James 3:12 – My brothers, a fig-tree is not able to produce olives or a vine fig! In this way neither a fountain produce salt and sweet <u>water</u>.

(31) 1 Peter 3:20 – to disobeying ones at some time, when at one time the long-suffering of the God waited in days of Noah, having prepared an ark, into which a few, this that is eight souls were saved through <u>water</u>.

(32) 2 Peter 3:5 – For this lay hidden from them determining that heavens were of old and earth from <u>water</u> and through <u>water</u> having subsided by the word of the God,

(33) 2 Peter 3:6 – through which at the time the world perished being flooded by <u>water</u>.

(34) 1 John 5:6 – This is the One coming through <u>water</u> and blood, Jesus, the Christ; not in the <u>water</u> only, but in the <u>water</u> and the blood. And the Spirit is the One testifying, because the Spirit is the truth.

(35) 1 John 5:8 – And there are three who bear witness in the earth, the Spirit and the <u>water</u> and the blood; and the three, they are into the one.

(36) *Revelation 1:15 – and His feet like burnished brass, having been fired in that manner in a furnace; and His voice in that manner of a sound of many <u>waters</u>;*

(37) *Revelation 7:17 – because the Lamb in the midst of the throne will shepherd them, and will lead them upon fountains of living <u>waters</u>, and the God will wipe off every tear from their eyes.*

(38) *Revelation 12:15 – And the serpent threw <u>water</u> out of his mouth in that manner of a river after the woman, in order that he might make her to be carried off by the river.*

(39) *Revelation 14:2 – And I heard a sound originating from the heaven in that manner of a sound of many <u>waters</u>, and in that manner of a sound of great thunder. And I heard a sound of harpers harping in their harps.*

(40) *Revelation 17:1 – And one came originating from the seven angels, the one having the seven bowls, and he spoke with me, saying to me, Come, I will show you the judgment of the great harlot, the one sitting upon the many <u>waters</u>,*

(41) *Revelation 17:15 – And he says to me, The <u>waters</u> which you saw, where the harlot sits, they are people and crowds and nations and tongues.*

(42) *Revelation 19:6 – And I heard in that manner a sound of a huge crowd, and in that manner a sound of many <u>waters</u>, and in that manner a sound of strong thunders, saying, Hallelujah! Because Lord, the God, the Almighty reigned.*

(43) *Revelation 21:6 – And he said to me, It has come into being. I am the Alpha and the Omega, the Beginning and the End. To the one thirsting, I will freely give from the fountain of the <u>water</u> of the life.*

(44) *Revelation 22:1 – And he showed me a clean river of <u>water</u> of life, bright in that manner of crystal, coming forth out of the throne of the God and the Lamb.*

(45) *Revelation 22:17 – And the Spirit and the Bride say, Come! And the one hearing says, Come! And the one thirsting come, and the one willing, take the <u>water</u> of life freely.*

- END -

WHY THE RELEASE OF THIS BOOK?

There appear to be equally as many "Christians" who believe "to be baptized in Holy Spirit" is different from "to be born from the Spirit" as opposed to many "Christians" who believe "to be baptized in Holy Spirit" is the same as "to be born from the Spirit."

There are also many "Christians" who believe that what the Lord Jesus Christ taught in John 6:5-61 concerning "eating His flesh and drinking His blood" is the partaking of the Lord's Table and consider this act an essential aspect of the gospel of salvation. Many other "Christians" do not share the same belief.

There are also "Christians" who continued the practice of washing the feet of other "Christians" to fulfil the commandment of the Lord Jesus Christ in John 13:4-17.

With such differences of understanding of the teachings and commandments of the Lord Jesus Christ how can believers come to a unity of the faith? In fact how do we know which practice and understanding is or are the truth?

Scriptures teach that a little leaven leavens the whole lump – meaning a little false teaching or false understanding of the truth will lead to the total contamination of the gospel of salvation.

It is for this reason that this book is released to reveal the truth concerning the issues as stated in this book to assist believers to be corrected in false or wrong understanding and hence wrong practice of the teaching and commandments of the Lord Jesus Christ, so that believers are truly set free from error to walk in the truth and that will lead believers to be overcomers to enter into the kingdom of the God.

Readers are urged to test the content in this book against the unadulterated word of the God, the original texts of the Bible in order to prove and/or to disprove its veracity.

Made in the USA
San Bernardino, CA
03 December 2016